RIPPLES IN THE POOL

The Rt Rev. R.A. Warke

MERCIER PRESS

Mercier Press Ltd
PO Box 5, 5 French Church Street, Cork *and*
24 Lower Abbey Street, Dublin 1

© The Rt Rev. R.A. Warke, 1993

ISBN 1 85635 - 064-9

A CIP catalogue record for this book
is available from the British Library.

Printed in Ireland by Colour Books Ltd.

Contents

Foreword

I HAVE LONG been convinced that some of the most useful and interesting insights into events come not from official reports or commentaries but from the pen of those who have lived through such events and, with the benefit of hindsight, can help us place faces and voices in perspective.

Bishop Roy Warke has extended this privilege to his readers in this book and we are in his debt for he writes with sensitivity and that crystal-clear appreciation of people which those of us who know him will always associate with his outlook. He takes us on a personal journey through a life of dedicated response to vocation. His ministry has extended during some of the most interesting years in the life of the Church of Ireland, and from his earliest days as a student prior to ordination, up to his present responsibilities as a bishop in the southern province, his reflections on events are both informative and significant. He writes with personal candour and his genuine interest in, and sympathy for, all sorts and conditions of people allow us to glimpse aspects of greater events which would otherwise be denied us. I have found his account of the happenings in the life of our Church take on a new significance as he places these happenings in the chronology of his own personal life and witness. The Church of Ireland is a relatively small Church family in which we all feel that we know each other so well, but when one member of that family places on paper his own reaction to the moving tapestry of events we gain even greater insight into what makes us what we are. Bishop Warke writes in a manner which allows the eye and mind to pass easily through some of the most significant happenings in our life as a Church and yet, on reflection, we are prompted to marvel yet again at how much has happened in our own generation to enrich and develop the Church we are seeking to serve.

I believe that this book will find a valued place on the shelves of all those who love Ireland and her Church and I hope that like me many will feel a new appreciation of the role of a bishop who has so obviously tried to apply his concept of the episcopate to the actual feelings, hopes and fears of ordinary people.

In commending this book I would thank Roy Warke for what he has given us not only in these words but by his friendship and service.

† Robert Armagh
The See House
Armagh
March 1993

Introduction

RIPPLES IN THE POOL might well have been sub-titled 'Memories and Musings'. I have drawn on some personal memories from the last forty years in the ministry of the Church of Ireland and mused on them in an equally personal way. No doubt others would have chosen differently. More time will be needed before the full impact can be analysed of these changing years on the life of the Church of Ireland. I gladly leave that to the professional historians.

A number of factors came together to lend impetus to the project, including the fortieth anniversary of ordination and the emphasis on telling the story which is part of the Decade of Evangelism.

I am deeply indebted to a number of people who helped jog my memory, in particular, Mr J.L.B. Deane (one of the honorary secretaries of the general synod) and Mr D.L. Phillips (clerk of the general synod). The encouragement of the Primate was greatly appreciated, as was his readiness to write a foreword. Mr Derek Johnston (Midelton College) cast an eye over the text and made many helpful suggestions. Mary Feehan of Mercier Press constantly encouraged and set attainable deadlines. Eileen, my wife, typed the script and her eagle eye corrected many a textual mistake. To all involved, I extend my thanks.

The Rt Rev. R.A. Warke

~ 1 ~

The Early Years

'WHERE DO YOU come from, Bishop?'

That question has been put to me many times in the last five years. Like most other fundamental questions it is not as simple as it first appears, and the answer sometimes depends on the audience!

In one sense it all began in Belfast just off the Lisburn Road on 10 July 1930. I'm told that the sound of Lambeg drums could be heard in the distance as men in shirt sleeves practised for the 'twelfth'. I probably didn't make the parade that year, but on many other occasions I watched for three hours, morning and evening, as the banners and the bands and the immaculately clad marchers made their way to and from the Field at Finaghy. Through the eyes of youth it was an unrivalled carnival of colour and sound. What a pity that youth must pass.

My initial stay in Belfast lasted for three weeks and then it was time to move south, to Mountmellick, in Laois, or Queen's County as it was still called at that time, where I lived for the next eighteen years. The only other time I have seen Mount-mellick mentioned in a book is in *Drink to the Bird* by Benedict Kiely. It's that kind of town. At least it was until the advent of Oliver Flanagan. And so, to the question, 'Where do you come from, Bishop?' what should I answer? What indeed, with a Belfast mother and a Donegal father (with three emigrant brothers) who made their home in a sleepy midlands town!

Of more importance, however, than where we come from

are the forces that influence our lives.

Growing up in the Ireland of the 1930s and 1940s was never easy. But, like most children, one was not aware of the difficulties. People appeared to be content with modest pleasures and the art of self-entertainment flourished. No doubt the 1937 Constitution made the headlines, but to a seven-year-old schoolboy the appearance of a battery-operated wireless was much more significant, especially when he sneaked down from bed to join a roomful of adults, in listening to a broadcast of one of Joe Louis' title fights.

The Second World War brought its own constraints. Rationing was severe in terms of food and clothes, while the use of 'the glimmer' for cooking outside the prescribed hours brought threats of dire consequences. The family's only concession to illegal trafficking was the few extra grains of tea sent in letters from Belfast. I can still recall Mick Kirwan the postman approaching with the letter and producing a sound like a muted castanet.

Of course Ireland was neutral during what was euphemistically described as 'the Emergency', but there was the constant threat of invasion by German parachute forces. We were all advised to dismantle our bicycles and blot out the names of towns. On one occasion a neighbour came rushing in to say that the parachute invasion had begun at Abbeyleix. It turned out to be the top of a haystack caught by the wind!

Nicholas Monsarrat in his book, *The Cruel Sea*, speaks of Ireland's 'smug neutrality', and one sometimes wonders if the subsequent course of Irish history would have been changed if we had in fact been invaded. Would a common enemy have drawn the people of this island closer together, or would ancient antagonisms have proved dominant?

What of religion in those early days in rural Ireland?

On the one hand, there was a type of pan-Protestant ecumenism, although the word 'ecumenism' still lay dormant. On the other hand, the vast majority of townspeople were Roman Catholic, presided over by a parish priest who regularly took his place in the local picture house to ensure that the purity of rural Ireland was maintained. There were Church of Ireland, Methodist and Presbyterian churches and a small group of

Quakers, a reminder that Mountmellick once had a Friends' secondary school. In addition to the regular Sunday worship, occasional united services were held in the YMCA hall. The hall was also the social focal point for the Protestant community – badminton and billiards and Protestant-only dances. Even a Roman Catholic taxi-driver would not be admitted.

To the modern generation it no doubt sounds intolerable, but at the time it was par for the course and reflected a very real ecclesiastical gulf. It was pre-Second Vatican Council, and *Ne Temere* ruled supreme. In order to survive, the Protestant community had little option but to lead a ghetto-style existence. Yet, strange to relate, there were good community relations. A certain way of life was almost expected from the Protestant community, not least in the sphere of Sunday observance. With a Northern Ireland background and a 1930s rural Ireland home, the distinctiveness of Sunday has been indelibly printed on my heart.

It was in such a setting that the first stirrings of vocation occurred. Indeed, today when sometimes asked by children in school when I first decided to be a clergyman, I have to reply that I can't remember a time when I didn't want to be one. I often envy those who have experienced a dramatic call to ministry. For me it was a gradual unfolding of the will of God nurtured by church-going, Sunday school, school and home. In an age when so much is of the instant variety, from coffee to comment, the Church is in danger of getting caught up in the syndrome, and not least as we face a future where the TV evangelist will have ready access to our homes.

The names of those who had a part to play in nurturing vocation will mean little to people outside Mountmellick, and even for the present generation they will have little relevance, but for one man they were inextricably bound up with his spiritual pilgrimage – Canon Godfrey Wilson (rector), James Guy (national school teacher) and Miss Bess Atkinson (Sunday school teacher). In their own way each one epitomised all that was and is best in the Church of Ireland.

For me, as for most Protestant young people in rural Ireland at that time, secondary education meant boarding school, just as it still does today. The choice lay between Kilkenny

College and The King's Hospital. Eventually as a result of the
persuasive powers of a clerical Old Boy, Canon Wilfred Bond,
I sat the entrance examination for The King's Hospital in June
1942, and at the beginning of the following September entered
the stately portals of the Blue Coat School in Blackhall Place,
Dublin, now the home of the Incorporated Law Society.

For those who are now accustomed to the comparative
luxury of modern boarding establishments it is difficult to
conjure up a picture of the frugality of the 1940s. Yet, despite
the constraints of rationing and the sparseness of the buildings, there was an atmosphere of loyalty engendered which
left an imprint for good on the lives of most pupils. Instrumental in this was, undoubtedly, the staff. Nowadays we talk glib-
ly of personal relationships, but in those days, no doubt helped by the small numbers (under 130), there was a very close
relationship between staff and pupils.

Ruling, and I use the word advisedly, over all that took
place, was the headmaster, the Rev. J.J. Butler, perhaps best
described as a benevolent despot. He had an intense loyalty to
the school, and an absorbing love for the school chapel. In a
real sense it was at the centre of school life, highlighted by
daily and Sunday worship. There, vocation to the ministry
was nurtured for many, not in any ostentatious way, but as
they experienced the dignity of Anglican worship, sang in the
choir, participated in the services and absorbed an ethos and
an atmosphere which, if difficult to define, was nonetheless
real. Small wonder that the ministry of the Church of Ireland
is liberally sprinkled with past pupils of The King's Hospital.
And not just the ordained ministry. Travelling around the
United Dioceses of Cork, Cloyne and Ross, I am deeply conscious of the number of KH past-pupils who play an active
role in parish life. That early exposure in the school chapel has
had a spin-off to the benefit of the whole Church. In the 1940s
the school was 'boys only' but now it is co-educational. If
events run true to form it will only be a matter of time before
the first Old Girl is ordained, now that the Church of Ireland
has taken a lead in this matter.

For those intending to enter the ministry forty years ago,
the natural progression was from secondary school to Trinity

College, Dublin. One entered the Divinity School after two years of the degree course. For the next two years, the degree and divinity courses ran parallel, with the final year devoted entirely to divinity.

Today candidates for the ministry must undergo a rigorous selection process. Following screening at the parish level, eventually, on the recommendation of the diocesan bishop, a candidate comes before the Central Advisory Council of Training for the Ministry (CACTM). From Monday to Friday tests and interviews take place and eventually, after close scrutiny and analysis, a recommendation is made to the bishop.

The contrast with forty years ago is quite startling. Then, it was a matter of filling in a small form with some personal details and replying to the question, 'Why do you want to be ordained?' But by and large it worked, and most of those coming to the end of their ministry at the present time, after a lifetime of devoted service to the Church of Ireland, are products of that system.

TCD at the end of the 1940s was an interesting place. There were still a number of ex-servicemen picking up the educational threads after the Second World War. The societies, sports clubs and faculties had an international mixture of students which greatly enriched the life of the university. In addition, Northern Ireland accents were prevalent. This geographical mixture compensated in some measure for the lack of Roman Catholic students resulting from the ban on entry imposed by the Roman Catholic Archbishop of Dublin. Since the ban was lifted, the religious balance has shifted. No doubt this has enriched the university in many ways, but those who were there in the immediate post-war decade enjoyed an experience which was unique.

Many divinity students lived in the Divinity Hostel in Mountjoy Square under the watchful eye of Michael Ferrar. By this time my family had moved to Dublin and because of this I was not compelled to live in 'The Hostel'. At the time, I welcomed this concession, but on hindsight I regret it. It gave to residents an opportunity to experience community and disciplined worship which to someone who was an only child would have been very valuable.

Although Sunday morning attendance at College Chapel was compulsory, I usually made it back to St John the Baptist, Clontarf in time to hear one of the finest preachers of the day, Canon J.B. Neligan, originally from Mountmellick.

At that time, divinity students were very much a part of university life, not least the various sports clubs including rugby, hockey, tennis, athletics, and even boxing. There is always a danger that those training for the ministry retreat into their ecclesiastical shell with a resultant double loss. They lose touch with the world in which they will have to exercise their future ministry, and also miss out on the opportunity to bring to bear on their own particular work environment the values for which they stand. As it was expressed by Archbishop Runcie at the 1988 Lambeth Conference, 'We are called to bring a gospel critique to the society in which we live'. The more contemporary term is 'kingdom values', including truth, justice, beauty and reconciliation. Like any other popular term, it too can become a cliché. However, it does contain within it a recognition that faith must be worked out where we are. Individual commitment to Jesus Christ must have a context within which it can grow and develop, otherwise it becomes stunted and mawkishly introspective.

The staff of the Divinity School in the late 1940s and early 1950s reads like a *Who's Who* of the Church of Ireland. Regius Professor was Canon J.E.L. Oulton assisted by Canon R.R. Hartford as Archbishop King's Professor, two contrasting personalities. Oulton, a bachelor, an introvert, a private person, who urged students not to marry while they were curates. Hartford, married to the Archbishop of Dublin's daughter, an extrovert, gregarious, the original Church of Ireland ecumenist, who urged students to marry early, as without a wife they were incomplete. At least one could quote an authority for whatever line of action one took!

It was the era of package theology, far removed from the seminar type of approach today. Questions at examinations were brief and factual, and students tended to regurgitate the notes given in lectures. In a sense, students were not meant to have opinions, or at least not meant to voice them in public. Lectures were meant to be absorbed and the dictum by which one lived was 'write it down'. Hartford in particular delighted to name drop and his quoting of authorities was liberally spiced with the catch-phrase, 'I knew him personally'. His premature death deprived the Church of Ireland of one of its characters. He evinced strong reactions from many of his contemporaries but none could doubt his devotion both to TCD and the Church of Ireland.

Dean of Residence and Lecturer in the Bible were G.O. Simms and R.G.F. Jenkins respectively. Some years later they were to prove a formidable pair as Archbishop and Archdeacon of Dublin.

Much has been written about George Simms who died in 1991, eleven years after he retired as Archbishop of Armagh. As Dean of Residence he was known for his encyclopaedic knowledge of students and their activities, and also as a deceptively stiff *viva voce* examiner. Those who did not pass invariably came away convinced that it was for their own good they should repeat the exam. Happily, 'the Archdeacon', as he is affectionately known, is still to be found in his accustomed pew in All Saint's, Grangegorman each Sunday. Those who succeeded him as Archdeacons of Dublin recall with gratitude the profitable sessions spent with him as they took up office. His knowledge of the Bible was matched only by his wisdom in the art of ecclesiastical diplomacy.

Ecclesiastical history was in the hands of Professor Jourdan, a much loved scholar whose lectures were not noted for their strict discipline. Sufficient to say that many a student received credit for attendance while pursuing less academic activities.

The Professor of Pastoral Theology was R.J. Kerr, rector of St George's, Dublin, and a man noted for his social conscience. His lectures were spiced with practical advice from his own experience of parochial life. Some of these pieces of advice were handed down by students from year to year, perhaps the best known being – 'You never know what you will be asked to do in parochial life. A man once asked me to get him a monkey, and Gentlemen, I got him a monkey.' It was only later on in the hurly burly of parish life that one began to appreciate the sound advice given by 'R.J'.

If the going was hard for the Professor of Pastoral Theology, it was even harder for the Rev. G.S. Nowlan, rector of Rathfarnham. To George Nowlan fell the task of training ordinands in reading the liturgy. A noted sportsman in his day, he was a quiet and patient man by nature, as I discovered a few years later when I served as his curate. But his patience must have been sorely tried as he sought to impart the elements of good diction to students who were less than responsive. Yet, how vital that aspect of ministry is, and I sometimes reflect on George Nowlan's efforts when I receive justifiable criticism of clergy who cannot be heard, even with the aid of modern loudspeaking systems. Indeed, in some ways these very systems have aggravated the problem because there is a real art in using amplification.

At another level, the intoning of services was taught by Canon J. Purser Shortt. Having started on this course, it is one of my regrets that I did not persist. Perhaps it was that by Friday afternoon the lure of the sports' field proved too great.

The sub-lecturers, as they were then known, were also parochial clergy – W.C. de Pauley, E.G. Daunt, E.W. Greening, W.C.G. Proctor, T.N.D.C. Salmon. In hindsight, they represented a remarkable body of men who had the capacity to combine parochial work with academic excellence. I cannot recall any of them ever missing a lecture, and on one occasion when Dean de Pauley, who sported flowing grey hair, was confined to barracks, his class gathered round his bed in St Patrick's Cathedral deanery. There can't have been too many lectures on the Thirty-nine Articles delivered in such a setting.

Our particular year was one of the smallest on record, just reaching double figures. I well recall Canon Greening surveying the class at an early stage and remarking, 'Never have so many owed so much to so few!' Even in the early 1950s the Church of Ireland was beginning to experience that shortage of ordinands with which we have been living ever since.

Saturday mornings were devoted to sermon composition. A text was supplied and two hours allotted for writing. Comments were made on the script by various members of the staff, and occasionally one had to preach. I still possess my first such sermon with the comments of George Simms written in that characteristic neat hand.

During the final divinity year, enquiries began to come in from rectors with vacant curacies. I'm not aware that there was a standard procedure, but the enquiries may well have been made to the Regius Professor in the first place.

I had three options – Derry, Belfast or Newtownards. I chose Newtownards under the Rev. R.J. Chisholm, and on Sunday, 5 July 1953, five days before my twenty-third birthday (necessitating a faculty), I was made a deacon in the Church of God by the Rt Rev. W.S. Kerr, Bishop of Down and Dromore.

~ 2 ~
The Church of 1953

1953 WAS A memorable year. Everest was conquered by Hillary and Tenzing, thereby removing one of the last challenges to human endeavour. The coronation of Queen Elizabeth II took place in June, and the showing of the subsequent film provided many a parish with an evening's enjoyment. Of greater significance, however, was the televising of the event (albeit on a limited scale) which proved to be a watershed in the field of communications. A new era was dawning which today is taken for granted by the younger generation.

The world at large was pondering the significance of the death of Stalin – would it herald a new age in East-West relations? Many years were to pass before the Berlin Wall was breached, and the Cold War was to be replaced by a series of localised conflicts giving the new-found freedom a tarnished look.

At the helm of the Church of Ireland was one of the great Church figures in this century, John Allen Fitzgerald Gregg. For forty-four years he exercised the office of a bishop and helped to guide the Church of Ireland through such traumas as two world wars, and the emergence of a new independent state. The consequent political polarisation has, on occasion, tested the reality of Anglican comprehensiveness, but the general synod each year is a reminder that divergent political philosophies can be embraced within the one Church tradition, and this in itself acts as a powerful apologia for the Christian faith.

Gregg's presidential address at the general synod of 1953 was a reminder that while much may change, much remains the same. Two of the main themes were candidates for the ministry and the maintenance and repair of churches. Forty years on, these are still topical subjects. At the pre-synod service in St Patrick's Cathedral the same year, the preacher was the Rev. Precentor A.A. Luce. Through him the Church of Ireland paid tribute to George Berkeley, Bishop of Cloyne (1734-53), one of its most famous holders of episcopal office, on the bicentenary of his death in 1753. It is said that when George Simms was appointed Bishop of Cork, Cloyne and Ross in 1952, he received a message from Luce – 'Congratulations on being elected Bishop of Cloyne.'

One of the major ecumenical advances of this century came about when the Church of South India was constituted in 1947. In 1953 the Church of Ireland, like many other Anglican Churches, was still vigorously debating what its relationship to the new body should be. Forty years on, the bishops of the C.S.I. are accepted within the Anglican Communion, and at the 1988 Lambeth Conference they played a full part.

In recent years liturgical revision has been an ever present factor in Church life. Even in 1953 there were faint indications of what was to come, with two bills before the synod to revise the services of baptism and confirmation. The former was lost at the second reading and the latter withdrawn. Later it was to be the perceived need for change at the local level which was to bring back baptism to the centre of the liturgical scene, and this, together with gathering international momentum, was the occasion of the setting up by the general synod in 1962 of the Liturgical Advisory Committee.

In 1953 the name of J.L.B. Deane first appeared on the general synod legislative scene. Having been elected in 1952 to represent the United Diocese of Cork, Cloyne and Ross, there has scarcely been a year since then when some piece of legislation has not been sponsored by him. Much of this has had to do with improving the pensions of clergy and their widows, and as chairman of the Church of Ireland Pensions' Board he has been responsible in large measure for the development of this unglamorous but vital part of the Church's work in recent years. Since 1970 he has been one the the general synod honorary secretaries. One year ahead of Barry Deane on the general synod scene was T.G. Stoney (elected in 1951), and together they have given over eighty years service to the highest legislative body in the Church of Ireland. This, together with their work at diocesan and parish level, is symbolic of the dedication shown by so many laity in the Church of Ireland.

In Dublin, bedecked for *An Tóstal*, Arthur William Barton was Archbishop. Recognised as an outstanding pastoral bishop, he is remembered by many, including the present writer for his confirmation addresses. I can still see him in the chapel of The King's Hospital as he moved easily up and down the aisle speaking words of practical wisdom in a delightful full voice. His book on confirmation preparation, *Further Instructed*, is still well worth reading. .

In 1944 the dioceses of Connor and Down and Dromore were separated. The bishop *in situ* was Charles King Irwin who retained the bishopric of Connor, while William Shaw Kerr was elected to Down and Dromore. Serving as an assistant curate in Down in the parish of St Mark, Newtownards, one was conscious of the contrasting reputations of the two men. King Irwin was a man of few words (or so his clergy reported), and conservative in his approach to ecclesiastical matters, while Kerr was scholarly, gentle and more liberal, although his reputation as a protagonist in the then very lively Roman Catholic controversy was well recognised. Nowhere was the contrast more obvious than in the matter of the remarriage of divorced people in church. Many a story is told of those who crossed the Lagan from the confines of Connor to avail of the more liberal attitude displayed by the Bishop of Down. The contrasting attitudes of two Church leaders are of interest as the general synod grapples with this emotive topic. Indeed it has been on the agenda for the past seventeen years through the select committee on the remarriage of divorced persons. Few committees can have made such an exhaustive study of their subject, and when decision time does come at the general synod it will be against a background of detailed knowledge and information – theological, denominational, historical, legal and geographical.

To enter the ministry in 1953 was to become part of an edifice which had about it an air of changelessness. As already mentioned, normal progression was from secondary school to university (usually TCD) for a primary degree, and thence to the Divinity School based in Trinity. There were a few mature students, usually picking up the threads having served in one of the forces in the United Kingdom. Married divinity students were a rarity and those entering the ministry were, by and large, a youthful breed. Even those who came into the ministry after working elsewhere – the bank or civil service, for example – were still comparatively youthful. Such was the case with my own first rector, Reginald Chisholm, who worked in the civil service for some years before coming to TCD. One suspects that those in other occupations were not exactly encouraged to consider the ministry if the words of Archbishop Gregg at the 1954 general synod are anything to go by. Making a plea for candidates for the ministry to come from the homes of the Church of Ireland, he said, 'Posts which involve dealing with things do not make the same call upon character as do those like the clerical life or the teacher's life'. The contrast today is quite remarkable with the youthful curate becoming more and more of a rarity.

Yet, as was always the case, there was wisdom in Gregg's words. It can be too easily assumed that experience of the world enhances performance in the ministry. Certainly, many an older candidate has brought invaluable experience to the ordained ministry, but unless it is refined by sensitivity to a whole new set of circumstances it can lead to inflexibility. Furthermore, without a percentage of younger clergy, the Church of Ireland is in danger of losing contact with its young people. I know of no better bridge between the institutional Church and the youth of today than a young cleric who is sensitive to youth. Whether we like to admit it or not, there is a generation gap, and unless we have clergy who can bridge that gap I fear it may become unbridgeable. Many a young curate has bemoaned the fact that he is expected to deal with young people. At times it can be frustrating, but in the long run it is time well spent.

Other contrasting aspects of ministry are worth recalling.

In 1953 the number of serving stipendiary clergy was 788; in 1993 it stands at 510. Then there were 132 retired clergy, now it is almost exactly double that number, 262. The auxiliary ministry did not exist in 1953 nor were there women in the ministry.

Forty years ago lay participation in worship was minimal. Very few licensed readers operated, and even readers of lessons at morning and evening prayer were not very plentiful. Today it is doubtful if the liturgical life of many dioceses could be maintained without the faithful service of readers, who are now uniformly trained to a high standard. In addition, many other lay people participate through reading lessons, leading intercessions and serving at Holy Communion.

In general, the role of women was negligible. They were permitted to be church-wardens, but I cannot recall one acting in that capacity. The same was true of licensed readers. It was rare to hear a woman reading a lesson, even at a Mothers' Union service.

Today the pendulum has swung sharply in the other direction and it is not uncommon to meet two lady church-wardens in a church, while the number of lady readers continues to rise. I believe it was this experience of women's ministry that helped to prepare the way for the acceptance of women priests at the 1990 general synod. For most people the issue is not one of theology but of practical application and ability. That I believe to be a fact of Irish parochial life, and it was reflected in the overwhelming lay vote at general synod.

It is also interesting to reflect on the conditions of service of the ordained person in 1953. The minimum stipend for rectors was £450, and curates usually started on £300 per annum out of which they had to pay for accommodation and all other expenses – hence the great affection for the bicycle. Retirement benefits were scarcely a factor in the equation, with the result that clergy often kept going into their eighties and even their nineties. For those entering the ministry today, the contrast is remarkable, and in addition to what has been accomplished by the Church authorities, clergy in the Republic came into the State Social Insurance scheme in 1975. The Church Pension Scheme has been the whipping boy at many a synod, both general and diocesan. It was designed (as once described by Bishop F.B. Moore) to enable retired clergy to live in reasonable comfort, and few would deny that the progress over the last number of years has seen that goal realised. Perhaps the ultimate accolade is the lack of negative criticism at general synod in recent years.

One other aspect of Church life forty years ago must be noted and that was the lack of certain church furnishings, and the plainness of clerical robes. No cross or candles were allowed on the Communion table, and coloured stoles were still a distant innovation. The more avant-garde risked a black stole!

Visitors from overseas found this phenomenon unusual, while at the same time invariably paying tribute to the solidity and solidarity of the Church of Ireland. Despite the lack of liturgical trimmings it was realised that the faith, once for all delivered to the saints, was in safekeeping.

~ 3 ~
Setting Out

A FIRST CURACY goes a long way towards determining a cleric's future attitude to ministry. In many ways it should be a furthering of the training received in theological college, equivalent to an extension of a fieldwork assignment.

So much depends on the rector involved and his ability to nurture his newly ordained colleague. For a curate it can be an enriching experience or something approaching a disaster. For me it was the former, and I look back on my two-and-a-half years in Newtownards as a time when many important lessons in ministry were learnt.

The omens were not always good. Shortly after my appointment a layman at the general synod, on hearing of my destination, remarked to my mother, 'Surely he's not going there'. I still don't know what he meant, unless it was related to a line from one of Joseph Tomelty's plays set in the Ards Peninsula, *Is the Priest at Home?* Referring to Newtownards, one of the characters remarks, 'Oh, that's the place where you could take all the virgins out in a wheelbarrow'.

If a first curacy is formative, the first week of a first curacy can sometimes set the headline for what is to follow. My first week witnessed two tragic deaths which called for pastoral care and sensitivity of the most demanding order, and this was exemplified by the rector, the Rev. R.J. Chisholm.

The first was a fifteen-year-old member of the parish scout troop, an only son, drowned in a Scottish lough, while at camp. To the rector fell the task of informing his parents and sister. I can think of few more demanding duties, yet it is the type of pastoral work so many clergy are called on to perform. Nor does it end with the bringing of sad tidings. There is the ongoing pastoral concern that is called for after the initial flood of sympathy has dried up. But the ripples of such a tragedy spread out to embrace a host of other people – scout leaders, fellow scouts, school pals – and all needed a measure of care and understanding as they tried to make sense of a seemingly senseless event. Tragedies never occur in isolation. There is always a context, and that context is the setting for the pastoral ministry.

The second tragic death was that of a well-known racing driver involved in a crash. At first he had appeared unhurt as he walked away from the scene on the circuit. But then he collapsed and died. A different set of circumstances, yet nonetheless making severe demands on the pastoral resources of the rector.

That first week was traumatic for a pale young curate, yet it underlined the shortness and uncertainty of human life, something which was to be a constantly recurring factor in succeeding years. So often it gives rise to the question 'WHY?' especially when the person concerned is in the springtime of life. Indeed, it is a question which dogs the footsteps of every cleric and forces him or her to come to grips with one of the great mysteries of our finite existence.

However, even when we have done our rationalising and perhaps placed a particular tragedy in the context of an imperfect world – in other words, when we have satisfied our own rational nature – we are still left with the task of commending our 'answer' to those nearest and dearest who are grieving the loss of a loved one. Others can distance themselves, but the clergy must remain alongside their people. Such is the nature of the pastoral ministry, and that first week taught me this lesson in a much more direct way than a year's lectures on pastoralia. At the time the deep end seemed very deep, but being in there taught one how to swim very quickly.

The ecclesiastical setting in Newtownards was an interesting one, to say the least of it. In addition to the Church of Ireland parish with 600 families, there were five Presbyterian churches, one Methodist church and a sample of every other branch of Protestantism imaginable. Added to these was a small Roman Catholic congregation.

There was a certain amount of pan-Protestant ecumenism involving the major Church traditions. For example, we came together to listen to relays of a Billy Graham crusade in London.

A major focal point was the preparation for a Bible Week to celebrate the 150th anniversary of the foundation in 1804 of the British and Foreign Bible Society. In addition to the physical preparations, we met in various churches each Sunday evening for prayer. Here one experienced the phenomenon of free-flowing extempore prayer in all its verbal glory. Someone said at the time that it was very much the battering ram approach at the gates of Heaven. As one who has tended to find God in the still small voice rather than the storm or earthquake, it was a novel experience.

Nevertheless, the Bible Week was an important and memorable event in the life of the community. It was conducted by Harding Wood, a noted biblical scholar, and some of the insights he left with us are still vivid in my mind. In particular, I recall one evening when he illustrated how the Bible speaks through a chapter, a verse or a word. On another occasion he drew our attention to Psalm 119, Verse 18 – 'Open thou mine eyes, that I may behold wondrous things out of thy law' – and suggested that each morning when reading a portion of scripture a 'W.T.', or Wonderful Thing, be taken from it and be recalled throughout the day. In such a way does the Bible come to life and its contents achieve relevance.

Memorable, but for less laudable reasons, was another event during that week. It had been left to me to organise a gathering for the primary schools of the town (the curate will look after the young people!) What better way than a film show related to the Bible? Whether it was the prospect of a free film show or a period off school, I don't know, but the brand new parish hall was packed to overflowing. However, for those used to a diet of cowboys and Indians and cops and robbers, what we had on offer was dull indeed. As unrest grew, we decided to cut our losses – educational and spiritual

– and abandon the show, much to the disgust of the patrons who were faced with returning to school earlier than intended. Some had to be 'gently' helped on their way, and while assisting one such pupil over the hall railings, I was bitten. For one fleeting moment I wondered if that man at the general synod hadn't been right after all! I have been bitten metaphorically many times since then, as is the lot of most clergy. I have even been bitten twice by dogs in people's homes (and superstition warns of a third time). But I could truly say at the time that Bible Week left an indelible mark on me.

At another level, the significance of the Bible was highlighted by the Primate, Dr Gregg, in his presidential address at the general synod – 'The Bible in our churches is not enough. The Bible must have its established place in our homes, and in the hearts of our people as individuals.'

One of the most descriptive phrases in use today regarding Northern Ireland is 'the two communities'. It is also one of the saddest because it indicates division of a complex nature involving religion, politics, history and culture. In the early 1950s the same division existed, but without the sustained viciousness that characterises life north of the border today. Others from within the situation are better placed to analyse current affairs. I can only look back and, in hindsight, try to interpret the signs as they existed forty years ago in a provincial town in Northern Ireland.

In some ways they mirror the scene as it exists for the Protestant population in the Republic of Ireland today, particularly with regard to numbers and the consequent minority mentality. The Roman Catholic congregation was small, very small. They existed in isolation. During my two-and-a-half years there I never once met a local Roman Catholic priest, not even when hospital visiting, which is often the place of contact. At the time this did not strike me as strange. It was normal for the climate of the day. On one occasion I was even advised not to buy sweets in a certain shop – it was owned by 'one of them'! The quality of sermons was often judged by the biblical texts quoted, while a controversial reference to the Roman Catholic Church earned bonus points.

This, however, was prior to the Second Vatican Council,

and as yet Pope John XXIII had not opened the windows to allow in the winds of change to disturb the attitude of triumphalism typified by such cries as 'Outside the Church there is no salvation', where the Church was understood as those in communion with Rome.

It is against this historical backdrop that one tries to understand something of the two-community mentality today. But could more have been done forty years ago to create a climate of tolerance? Looking back one is conscious of a docile acceptance of the status quo. But it was compounded by the conditions of the day and few, if any, had the capacity to gaze into the crystal ball and see the dark shadow emerging on the horizon. Violence, when it did rear its ugly head in the 1950s, tended to be isolated without the international sophistication of today.

The parochial ministry has largely to do with being a faithful steward, not least of time. It is not unlike playing a game. If one doesn't get the basics right, there is no point in attempting the more difficult manoeuvres. Much of the work is routine and follows a pattern, week by week, involving such matters as worship, visiting, reading, sermon preparation, organisations. Newtownards was a good training ground in this work. Through the years I have tried to maintain the systematic habits cultivated in that first curacy, especially with regard to visiting, and pass them on to the colleagues with whom I have had the privilege of working. In the Swinging Sixties, visiting received a bad press. More sophisticated methods of group communications were advocated by the rising generation of curates. But there is no substitute in the Irish context for the pastoral visit to the home. It opens up avenues of communication that will remain closed in any other setting, not to mention the obvious message of concern it conveys. Even in the Decade of Evangelism when we are encouraged to look outwards, we must be careful not to neglect the pastoral needs of regular parishioners.

The danger with routine is that it will become monotonous and end up being neglected. One way to avoid this pitfall is to add variety. For me variety took the shape of a summer course at St Augustine's College, Canterbury, in 1955. At that time, St Augustine's was regarded as the central college of the Anglican Communion, and it specialised in courses with an international flavour. The warden was Canon C.K. Sansbury who was later to become Bishop of Singapore. One of the students was the Rev. E. Sabiti, who attended under the auspices of the Church Missionary Society. I well recall spending some hours with him as he agonised over his future, and many years later I was fascinated to discover that he had become an African archbishop of great courage.

Two Americans on the course became close friends, the Rev. Sam Wylie and Dan Sullivan. Sam later became head of General Seminary, New York, and while there conducted a memorable mission in Zion Parish, Dublin, where I was rector. He next was elected Bishop of Northern Michigan, but died very suddenly on a return visit to General. He had a great love for the Church of Ireland, and visited this country many times to experience what he regarded as a balanced form of Anglicanism. Dan was ordained shortly after returning to America from Canterbury. He spent an early period of his ministry in Rangeley, Maine, before moving to the Church of the Good Shepherd in Paoli, Pennsylvania.

One of the lecturers on the course was Professor Pearson Parker, an American New Testament scholar. He was a man of contrasting personality. Away from the lecture room he was quiet in the extreme – shyness personified. In the lecture room his personality was transformed and he became one of the most dynamic speakers imaginable.

Each morning there was a celebration of Holy Communion using the form of service appropriate to a particular part of the Anglican Communion. When it came to Ireland's turn I decided to use the full form of the commandments. It turned out to be a rare occurrence for those present and they valued the opportunity to hear the familiar words in the context of the Church's highest act of worship. Many would contend that the Church in general has done society a disservice in recent years by the neglect of the commandments in public worship. One of the good features of the 1984 *Alternative Prayer Book* is the opportunity to use the New Testament summary alongside the commandments themselves.

St Augustine's was just across the road from Canterbury Cathedral, and students occasionally acted as guide assistants. Processing with cross and candles, duly garbed, one secretly hoped that no Irish visitors would appear! It was before the more open approach to such matters today. But the cathedral and the college did open a window on the Anglican world and helped to broaden horizons which up until then had been severely confined. The lesson of interaction is an important one to learn, whether it be between traditions within Anglicanism, or between different churches and communities.

Looking back over the years on that Canterbury experience, I can see in it the first of a subsequent series of events that were to affect my ministry. Chance meetings that turn out to be significant are seldom as random as they first appear. Such was certainly true of my meeting with Sam Wylie who was to reappear at important points of decision over the years

Two international gatherings were held in the summer of 1954 – the Anglican Congress at Minneapolis and the meeting of the World Council of Churches at Evanston. As is so often the case, the impact at local level was minimal. I have long since felt that representation at such gatherings should not become solidified as it often does, but should be spread amongst as many people as possible and changed frequently. This at least enables a variety of representatives to gain a vision of the Church beyond their own immediate setting, with the possibility of sharing that vision to the benefit of all concerned. The Church of Ireland was honoured at Minneapolis when Archbishop Barton preached at the closing service and, with typical candour, reminded delegates of the priorities of the Church based on the questions put to candidate priests at the ordination service.

One of the events coming back into vogue at present is the parish mission. It appears that the Decade of Evangelism has been instrumental in placing this form of activity on the parochial agenda once again, and some dioceses are promoting simultaneous missions in every parish. This occurred in Dublin as a means of celebrating the centenary of disestablishment. It begged the question as to the appropriateness or otherwise of holding a series of missions at the one time. Are all parishes likely to be ripe for mission at the same time?

There are, of course, different forms of mission, perhaps best illustrated by the words of the prayer in the *Book of Common Prayer* for a Parochial Mission – 'Arouse the careless ... humble the self-righteous, soften the hardened, encourage the fearful, relieve the doubting, bring many souls in loving faith and self-surrender to thyself, and visit us with thy salvation'.

I mention this matter of parochial mission because, in many ways, it dominated my time in Newtownards. It was deemed that the parish would benefit from such an event, with an evangelistic emphasis. After much thought and prayer a missioner was appointed, the Rev. Jack Nichols, a gifted speaker, who had a fascinating ability to deal each evening with questions from the congregation. Preparation for the mission was thorough and lasted for a year, involving briefing visits from the missioner. Indeed it was said, and I have heard it repeated since, that preparation for a parochial mission should be of such a nature that should the missioner be unable to come at the last moment, that parish would not be deprived of benefit and blessing. One feature of Jack Nichols' ministry was the titles he chose for his addresses. One such title was 'Pigs for Prosperity' and consisted of a sermon based on the story of the Gaderene Swine. I will leave the reader to work out the content!

The impact of such an event is difficult to measure. For the cynical it was a mere pandering to the emotions of the spiritual vagabonds in the parish. Did not Northern Ireland suffer from a surfeit of missions? Yet, for those who had ears to hear, there was an undoubted challenge presented in a direct but balanced manner. I don't recall a dramatic increase in church attendance, but there is no doubt that for many people it was a time when faith was deepened, and for some it marked the rekindling of dying embers.

As with all such events there is a danger that the personality takes over. But such was not the case with Jack Nichols. He faithfully presented Christ crucified and bore testimony to John the Baptist's words – 'He must increase, but I must decrease.'

A parish is basically its people. That may seem a trite

comment, but it is nonetheless true and sometimes forgotten. As I recall those early years in the ministry and the people with whom I came in contact, and as I look at the situation today, I cannot help but reflect that Jesus hadn't very much trouble with the ordinary people of his day, it was with the leaders; and it was only when people were manipulated by their leaders that trouble really started.

I learnt much from the ordinary people of my first curacy. Let me explain:

MAY was one of the first people I visited after being ordained. I went along to the house resplendent in a new suit and dog collar, bubbling over with all the theories of pastoral visiting imparted in the lecture room. I discovered an old lady, bent up and completely crippled with what a native Dubliner was later to describe as 'the auld ariteritus'. For years she had been confined to a wheelchair and cared for by a devoted daughter.

Despite her painful and crippling illness, May was one of those rare people who are able to spread an aura of happiness and contentment all around them. You would feel it as soon as you entered the room. If anyone had good cause to bemoan her lot it was she, but over the next couple of years I was to gain much more from her by way of spiritual insight than she could ever have gained through me.

The whys and wherefores of human suffering have perplexed people from the dawn of time. For me, May was one of the first people to lift the subject out of the theory of the lecture room. There is no doubt that her education would have stopped far short of the classics, but she gave real significance to an old Latin tag which means 'Solve the problem of suffering by suffering'.

JOHN was an elderly senior citizen. I met him one day as I was walking down the street about a year after being ordained. I knew he was a parishioner but had no recollection of seeing him in church. We got chatting, and eventually I asked him why he didn't come to church. 'I'll tell you why,' he said, in a typically blunt forthright manner. 'It's because you clergy never preach a sermon on the Book of the Revelation.' I was tempted to remark – 'How do you know if you never come?' but instead, knowing there was a grain of truth in what he said, replied, 'You know, that's something I've always intended to do.' He looked me straight between the eyes and replied, 'Young man, the road to Hell is paved with good intentions.'

The story had a happy ending. I managed, after much burning of the midnight oil, to write a sermon on the Book of the Revelation. John duly came to church on the appointed Sunday – and kept on coming! We became good friends, and remained so until time eventually took its toll and he was laid to rest.

All that happened some years ago, but I have never forgotten the phrase he used with such telling effect at our first meeting – 'The road to Hell is paved with good intentions'. I often think of it today when I hear someone say – 'I'll give you a ring' or 'I'll be with you first thing in the morning'.

Old **BILL** was a remarkable character, indeed he was unique. He lived on his own in a small three-roomed house in a back street, which had the distinction of being the last house in the town to have a hand loom in it for weaving tweeds. The area was noted for its linen work, for its knitwear, and over the years for its tweeds, hand-woven in the homes of the people. I don't suppose it was called a cottage industry in those days, but the idea was the same.

However, times change. New methods are introduced to speed up production, and the individual craftsman gets swallowed up. I don't know how Bill would have survived in today's world of basic wages, percentage increases, productivity deals and differentials, but I am glad I was there to have seen something of another era. The care Bill gave to his machine, the pride he took in his work, the individual attention he seemed to give to each thread, all added up to workmanship of the highest order. I sat and watched spellbound on numerous occasions as his whole personality appeared to be involved in the work, and his hands and feet moved in perfect harmony. I don't suppose he ever heard the expression 'job satisfaction', but simply to watch him at work gave real meaning to that phrase, even though it would have been impossible to measure in today's terms.

Such were the ordinary people of a typical northern parish, and for me it was a privilege to serve them. By and large, their successors, like them, want nothing more than to be allowed to live at peace with their neighbours and earn an honest living.

~ 4 ~

Southward Bound

OFTEN IT IS non-ecclesiastical factors that determine the direction clerical lives take. As I came to the end of two-and-a-half years in Newtownards it became obvious that the health of my father was deteriorating. Alas, there were no by-pass operations in those days to give a new lease of life. At the same time, a vacancy occurred in the curacy of St Catherine's Parish, Dublin, and after much heart-searching I moved south taking up duty on 1 January 1956. Three weeks later, my father died.

The Church of Ireland in Dublin in the mid-1950s boasted thirty-five curates, and one of the happy memories is of the regular monthly meetings for junior clergy in the Missions to Seamen building on Eden Quay. They were stimulating occasions and, in addition to the intellectual and spiritual content, afforded an opportunity for fellowship much appreciated by one who had recently returned to the diocese.

The diocese was headed by Archbishop Barton who was to retire later that year. He was succeeded by George Simms, translated from Cork after a spell of just four years. Election was by the diocesan synod and there was little doubt where the wishes of the House lay.

Archbishop Gregg was still in Armagh, which meant that the Church of Ireland then had both the oldest and youngest archbishops in the Anglican Communion.

At the 1956 general synod a bill was passed to set up the Sparsely Populated Areas Commission (SPAC). Speaking of the first report of the commission the following year, Gregg said – 'It presents us with one of those calls for readjustment which the changes of time impose upon what we mistakenly fancy to be a settled economy'. How true his words were, yet how slow many are to grasp their relevance even today when change is, if anything, more rapid. The difficult work of the commission was carried out under the chairmanship of the late Frank Jacob.

Within the Church of Ireland there is an attachment to buildings. Perhaps, given our minority status, this is not un-natural. They provide tangible evidence of our presence. But this must be weighed against such factors as the cost of maintenance, ability to staff them and ease of modern transport. SPAC did its best to deal in a realistic manner with an ongoing problem, and when its span of life came to an end in 1965, while many sighed with relief, others acknowledged the value of the work done.

In 1958 an unusual feature of church life was the appointment of three bishops – Alan Buchanan to Clogher, Arthur Butler to Tuam and Cecil de Pauley to Cashel. Those who had studied under de Pauley in the Divinity School were conscious of his depth of learning and spirituality and also his sense of humour. He and I had a common clerical acquaintance in America, and on one occasion, when driving with him to a service on Long Island at which the bishop was to preach, he turned and said, 'Will I preach the Gospel or tell them about St Patrick?'

The other two bishops were military men but of contrasting personalities. Alan Buchanan, who had been rector of Bangor and a very helpful neighbour to the clergy in Newtownards, came under the influence of G.A. Studdart Kennedy, 'Woodbine Willie', and brought a deep social conscience to his ministry. At the popular youth conferences of that period his name was most likely to be chosen for the 'Christian and Work' slot. Butler, having served under Montgomery in North Africa, carried a Monty-like precision into his ministry. While rector of Monkstown, he delivered a series of Sunday evening addresses on the boy meets girl theme (Jack and Jill). Each night he broke off just as the relationship was reaching a crucial point. The result was a full church each Sunday in anticipation of the unfolding drama. Nowadays, serials such as *Glenroe* and *Coronation Street* use the same ploy to retain audience interest. The series received an accolade of sorts when there appeared a mock examination paper, circulating among the divinity students of the day and based on those addresses.

Right from the time of disestablishment in 1870, the laity of the Church of Ireland have had a significant role to play. At parochial, diocesan and national level they are involved, and this involvement is often held out as a contribution in the ecumenical sphere. But it is a limited type of involvement centring on administration. For example, at local select vestry level we refer to 'the three Fs' – finance, furnishings and fabric – and, constitutionally speaking, there the matter rests. Again, at general synod level, it is administration that so often dominates proceedings.

It was at the 1958 general synod that Archbishop Gregg reflected on this issue: 'What is the reason for all this business – these reports and accounts? I would answer that the ultimate purpose of it all is to witness to God.' Perhaps we witness to God not so much by *what* we do as *how* we do it in the councils of the Church. There is a need for us to incarnate the mind of Christ. Fourteen years later in 1972, again at the general synod, Archbishop Simms in his presidential address returned to the same theme when he said: 'May our Church's business always be seen to be our Master's business; where we fail in this, may we be forgiven and granted opportunities of starting on fresh lines.'

The matter was brought up to date at the 1988 Lambeth Conference when, in the context of the Decade of Evangelism, a call went out to transform diocesan and local church structures (Resolution 44). Archbishop Runcie put the challenge succinctly when he said at the same conference: 'We are called to bring a gospel critique to the society in which we live.'

Few Lambeth Conference reports have been more frequently quoted than that of 1958 and, in particular, part of the section dealing with 'The Family in Contemporary Society'. This segment has figured prominently in the Church of

Ireland's position statements on the subject of abortion. Usually just a few lines from the appropriate paragraph are noted, and so it may be of interest to quote the whole paragraph:

> In the strongest terms, Christians reject the practice of induced abortion, or infanticide, which involves the killing of a life already conceived (as well as a violation of the personality of the mother), save at the dictate of strict and undeniable medical necessity. The plight of families, or, indeed of governments, trapped in hopeless poverty and over-population, may well help us to understand why they think abortion more merciful than the slow starvation which looms ahead. Still, the sacredness of life is, in Christian eyes, an absolute which should not be violated.

At the time few people could have envisaged the emotive nature of the debate that would ensue in 1983 and again, to a lesser extent, in 1992 when the country was faced with referenda calculated to confuse rather than resolve an issue of such intense human concern. As events were to prove, the Church of Ireland was wise in its warning that such matters should not be dealt with by way of referendum, but rather by legislation.

The parish of St Catherine had a proud history. At the turn of the century it was one of the leading parishes in Dublin. St Victor's church was built to cater for expanding numbers, and the parish school in Donore Avenue was a flourishing institution. By 1956 the situation had changed dramatically. The growing suburbs were siphoning off the inner city congregations as people moved to new housing areas, especially on the south side of the city. In addition, emigration was rife, and in one particular week thirty-nine people left the parish, mostly bound for Canada which was the mecca for many who found employment difficult to obtain in their own country. Among those who left were many graduates, especially engineers. A number of clergy also found their way to Canada in the 1950s, and the diocese of Huron was particularly well staffed with Irishmen. Some eventually were elected to the Canadian House of Bishops and at the 1988 Lambeth Conference it was a great joy to meet Bishop John Conlin of the diocese of Brandon whose roots were in Down diocese.

The rector of St Catherine's was the Rev. Norman Commiskey, whose father had been headmaster of Morgan's School, Castleknock. He himself had been a noted athlete when in Trinity. It was not an easy task being rector of an inner city parish. Little could be done to halt the inevitable decline in numbers, and with it the sense of fatalism that the Church of Ireland was on the way out.

For long, we have stressed the role of the parish as the location where the real work of the Church is carried out – the coalface so to speak. It is the place where faith must find its fulfilment in action. The diocese may be the administrative hub, but it is in the parish that the real work is done. Given this emphasis, it is inevitable that when the parish begins to decline, the overall perception of the Church begins to suffer also.

Despite this, we did manage to maintain a fairly vibrant parochial life with the help of loyal and enthusiastic parishioners. There was a genuine consciousness of the heritage into which we had entered. This, of course, can have the negative effect of maintaining the status quo at all costs, and no doubt there was some of that present. But without it the incentive for survival is diminished.

During that time the parish was looked at by the City and Town Parishes Commission – the city equivalent of SPAC. It had the effect of rallying the parochial forces, and it was not until a few years later that positive action was taken during the incumbency of the Rev. (now Canon) Dick Bertram. For the moment, services remained unaltered, even to the extent of Sunday evening worship in St Catherine's with a regular congregation of organist, sexton, clergyman and Mrs Cleary, dressed in black and sitting behind a pillar – and that in a church built to house close on a thousand. It was only when the building became dangerous because of falling masonry that it experienced some experiments in community use, apparently without success.

Nevertheless, I often think of those Sunday evening services, where two or three were gathered together, as I walk along Thomas Street on my way to catch the Cork train at Heuston Station. I think of the pigs that used to be tossed into the graveyard and the calls to the health department of Dublin Corporation. I think too of the complex aroma of coffee, brewery and knackers' yard that regularly assailed the nostrils of parishioners. Nor was history enshrined only in the church building itself. On the street outside it, stood a stone commemorating the execution of Robert Emmet.

As is so often the case in inner city parishes there were various funds and trusts with which the clergy were involved. St Catherine's Trustees, including the archbishop, archdeacon and rector, were responsible for a variety of properties in the area, many of them more a liability than an asset. The Meath Loan Fund, of which the curate was a member, was responsible for disbursing modest sums of money to the locals, often for the purpose of setting up in the pig business. At certain times of the year we also distributed red flannel to help keep out the winter cold. On this committee was the minister of Donore Presbyterian church, the Rev. G.B.G. McConnell, a man of firm convictions and a noted controversialist. It is a sign of changing times that his church is now a mosque serving the growing Muslim community in Dublin.

The area between St Catherine's and St Victor's contained St Theresa's Gardens, a large complex of Corporation flats. It was one of those housing experiments which, in many areas, proved to be a disaster. Little or no thought was given to the provision of recreational facilities, with the result that the many children in the flats simply turned to vandalism. We had one family living in the complex, and to their credit they maintained the highest standards of homemaking, and were, I believe, an example and inspiration to many of their neighbours. But it was not easy.

The gardaí were constantly involved, and one man in particular achieved a remarkable degree of respect. He was known locally, and indeed nationally as 'Lugs' Branagan – I think his Christian name was Jim. He was a big man with prominent ears, as the nickname would suggest, but his presence was enough to restore law and order to the most threatening situation. Perhaps the fact that he was involved deeply with amateur boxing and was an international referee often to be seen at the National Stadium on the South Circular Road (near St Victor's Church), had something to do with it. Certainly reading of his death in the national press not so very long ago brought back a flood of memories of St Theresa's Gardens and the National Stadium.

The parochial organisations in the parish were of a regular nature such as Mothers' Union, Men's Club, Youth Club and Boys' Brigade. But overshadowing everything else was the Girls' Brigade. At the time it was reckoned to be quite simply the best company in Ireland. Each year a plethora of cups and shields came its way. It was under the captaincy of Connie Hall, who was also brigade secretary. Her dedication to the Girls' Brigade was total and this commitment was communicated to an outstanding group of officers. My first contact with the company on coming to the parish was to enter the parochial hall rather noisily as tests were taking place for the All-Ireland Senior Solo competitions. Miss Hall was not amused! However, she forgave me and we became firm friends and she did much to teach me the value of good leadership for young people. Her girls would have done anything for her – or almost anything. Of her that overused expression could in truth be used – she became a legend in her own lifetime.

During my time at St Catherine's an event took place which was to turn out to be a portent for the future; a cloud no bigger than a man's hand. In 1956 the Hungarian uprising occurred, that brave but abortive attempt to break out from Soviet domination. Many people did escape to the West and some found their way to Ireland. The Hungarian Relief Fund came to be the focus for people's charitable instincts, not unlike Somalia today. Various events were run to help the fund, some of them involving sports clubs. The hockey club to which I belonged decided to play a charity match against the Rest of Leinster. It was arranged for a Sunday, but as a member of the home team this posed a problem. I questioned the value of playing the match on a Sunday, but was assured that this would be a once-off event in a good cause. Nevertheless, I decided not to play, and have stuck to that principle ever since.

There is no need to elaborate on the way Sunday sport has developed in the intervening years. It has become the accepted norm, and I believe has had a detrimental effect on the life of the Church of Ireland. It has diminished the concept of Sunday as the Lord's Day and placed pressures on many of our young people in relation to church attendance. This is the message coming through from a number of clergy, some of whom are keen sportsmen themselves. In a secular age this may not be a matter of great importance to many people – simply an accepted pattern of modern life. Yet, I believe it is chipping away at the spiritual fibre of modern society, certainly where the Church of Ireland is concerned. Archbishop Gregg in his wisdom once said, 'A God unworshipped is a God unknown', and where a stumbling block is put in the way of worship those who do so should think seriously of the end result. The Church needs its young people to add vibrancy to its worship. It is not just a matter of filling pews, but of the offering of worship by the whole people of God.

Periodically, an individual does take a stand. At the heart of the Oscar-winning film *Chariots of Fire* in 1981, was the story of Eric Liddle whose stand on Sunday involvement at the Olympics of 1924 caused such consternation among the British officials. Although the story was from another era, it was fascinating that it should have gripped the attention of modern sophisticated audiences around the world. Perhaps a clue to the reason can be found in an interview given at the time by the film's script writer, Colin Weldon. Weldon said that at first sight it was the most unlikely material for a box-office success. But he went on to say that gradually, as he began to get inside the minds of the main characters, he came to be aware of the power that motivated them. At the end of the interview he was asked, 'What would you say is the message of the film – what is it trying to say?' He paused for a moment and then replied – 'I think its real message is that there is a spiritual dimension to life.'

A more modern example is Michael Jones, the All Black rugby player who does not turn out on Sundays. By all accounts, he is one of the best players in the world and a vital cog in the All Blacks machine. But his principles are respected, even when it means sitting on the sidelines at a vital world cup match.

In our comparatively small Church of Ireland community we need to be careful that we don't shoot ourselves in the foot. If, as is often said, in order to compete at the highest level we must eat into the sanctity of Sunday, then surely there is a responsibility to recognise the distinctiveness of the day, and as far as possible cater for what, by tradition, is the distinctive activity of that day, the worship of Almighty God.

At a time when major steps have been taken to upgrade the stipends of clergy and their entitlements, it is interesting to reflect on the situation of a curate in 1956. The move from Newtownards to St Catherine's involved a drop in stipend, from £350 per annum to £325, and £25 of this was in payment for emptying the ESB meters in the parochial hall and school.

To be in St Catherine's in the 1950s and taking note of the neighbouring rectors was to be conscious of the evangelical tradition in the Church of Ireland at that time. In St Kevin's, regarded as the flagship of the evangelicals, was John Smallhorn. In the vestry of the church was a notice urging those taking services to refrain from wearing a cassock. A floor-length surplice was the order of the day, but I never officiated there without being conscious of the words of the psalmist – 'The Lord delighteth not in any man's legs'. Later, as archdeacon, I was present at the last service to be held in the church before closure – a very moving occasion with a genuine feeling of thanksgiving despite the sadness and the occasional tear.

Rector of St Luke's was Cecil Williams, small in stature but large in conviction, who has been fearless in his public championing of biblical ethical principles. Completing a formidable trio was Cecil Proctor in Harold's Cross. For many he was the voice of Protestantism and his letters were a feature of many a correspondence in *The Irish Times*, not least in relation to the mixed marriage controversy. Later, in 1972, it was my privilege to have him as my curate for five months before he retired from the active ministry. It was a very rewarding experience, and the calibre of his character was such that at no time did I feel a sense of inferiority, despite his fund of learning and wide pastoral experience. When he died in 1992 the Church of Ireland lost one of its best known and most illustrious sons.

The parish with which we had most contact was St James',
and the two parishes were later to be amalgamated. The rector
at the time was Chancellor James Alcock whose wife, Ruth,
was a much loved doctor in the area. The canon was coming to
the end of his active ministry but still retained the devotion
and affection of his parishioners, despite the frailty of the
flesh. It was in the days before early retirements and, during a
lengthy incumbency, a firm bond had been built up between
priest and people.

Today the pendulum has swung in the opposite direction,
and clergy in general are grateful for the opportunity to lay
down the burdens of office at a much earlier age. Perhaps the
burdens are greater, certainly they are more complex. But even
if the balance is tipped heavily in favour of early retirement
we should never lose sight of the merits of the older system. It
retained within the structures of the Church a deal of accu-
mulated wisdom which is not easily acquired. Occasionally it
caused a blockage in promotion, and having served for eleven
years as a curate I am as conscious of this as anyone. Yet, having tackled our administration in such a practical and professional manner, I sometimes wonder if we have not diminished
our pastoral capacity.

The geographical area embraced by St Catherine's parish
was steeped in history. It incorporated part of the Liberties
and bordered on the Coombe, immortalised by Jimmy O'Dea
in the song 'Biddy Mulligan, the Pride of the Coombe'. The
cobble stones evoked images of a bygone age – as well as
being murder on a bicycle! The people were the salt of the
earth, kindly and direct with a typical Dublin sense of humour. Cork Street ran through the middle of the parish and
for most people this spoke of one thing only – the fever hospital. By the mid-1950s this had changed and the hospital had
become an old people's home. The civic authorities provided a
delightful chapel for the Protestant patients which was formally opened with due ceremony. In the midst of decline, it
was a small oasis of growth. Each Wednesday morning there
was a service attended by a group of real characters. What a
wonderful miscellany of Dublin life would have unfolded if
only their stories had been recorded.

In the summer of 1958 I was approached and asked if I would join Canon George Nowlan on the staff of Rathfarnham parish. On the basis that a contrast in ministry is good for experience, on All Saints' Day 1958 I took up duty as curate-assistant in what was then the largest parish numerically in the south of Ireland, with 600 families.

~ 5 ~

Suburbia

EVEN IN 1958, Rathfarnham village retained some of its rural characteristics. Many of the shops had a typical olde worlde atmosphere far removed from the modern supermarket. The parish school had an open fire, one teacher and a handful of pupils. The local church in the centre of the village was built to cater for a limited congregation.

But change was on the way, symbolised by the ever increasing volume of traffic through the Main Street. That title in itself told a geographical story of days before such addresses as Dublin 14.

I celebrated Holy Communion at 8 o'clock on that first All Saints' morning, and in the vestry before the service made contact with one of the parish characters – the sexton. I cannot recall him being referred to as anything but Acton. Perhaps it was a lesson in local social history.

One of the most useful pieces of advice I received on entering the ministry was to keep on the right side of the sexton – that was in the days when most parishes had a sexton. Certainly in Rathfarnham he was a power in the land, and the organisations using the Rathfarnham Memorial Hall stepped out of line at their peril. On that first morning in the parish I commented on the merit of the clock in the vestry, an ancient time piece which added character to the room. I was met with the retort: 'It's the only thing that works around here!'

In addition to the contrast involved in going to Rathfarnham, I looked forward to working with George Nowlan. For me he typified all that was best in the parochial ministry of the Church of Ireland. A shy man, yet he was what one of his friends, Giles Blennerhassett, described as 'a quiet revolutionary'. During the next five years I was to discover the truth of that description. In his young days he had been a noted cricketer and rugby player for Clontarf, and he never lost his zest for games. For many years he was a selector of the Trinity 2nd XV (he used to say that was where you saw the best rugby), and was honoured by being made president of Dublin University Football Club in the early 1960s.

As we moved into 1959 some interesting developments were taking place on the wider Church scene. On 25 January Pope John XXIII, who had been Pope for just ninety days, announced his plan to convene an ecumenical council (an interesting title by today's standards). It was to lead to almost four years preparation and the opening of what came to be known as Vatican II on 11 October 1962.

Archbishop Gregg retired after forty-four years as a bishop, and speaking at the general synod that year his successor, James McCann, paid this tribute: 'Throughout it all His Grace was a wise guide, patient, fair, rock-like in principle, a great public figure in Irish life, equally trusted and loved north and south.'

At the same general synod a bill was passed to allow for the setting up of episcopal electoral colleges. By moving appointments away from diocesan synods and by introducing more diverse representation, it was hoped that the wider interest of the Church would be taken into account. It is of interest that of the twelve members of the present House of Bishops (December 1992) only two were initially chosen for the dioceses in which they were then serving.

Also in 1959 the building of St Anne's Cathedral, Belfast, was brought a stage further by the consecration of the eastern apse and ambulatory. It is a majestic building, and today in the period of strife it stands as a striking witness to better things, and to the deep-rooted faith of those who worship there. It is also a centre of ecumenism in an area where response to the divine imperative is viewed by many as a sign of ecclesiastical weakness. Having been invited to deliver the ecumenical spring lecture there in 1989, it was something of an experience to be greeted on arrival on the steps of the cathedral by a group of protesting hymn singers led by 'Big Ian' himself.

During my early days in Rathfarnham we were joined on the staff by another colleague, and the parish enjoyed the rare luxury of a rector and two curates. But the second curate was an unusual person, and if I had to name the most unforgettable character I ever met, the Rev. John Jackson would certainly be in line for the title.

Having retired as supervisor of the telephone service in Dublin, he then persuaded Archbishop Simms that he had a few years left in him to give to the Church in whole-time service through the ministry. He took the Diploma in Biblical Studies at TCD, and at the age of sixty-eight was ordained. A book could be written about the following five years. John had his roots in rural Ireland with a distinctive accent to prove it. As he delighted in saying to those more used to the richer tones of south Dublin suburbia, 'You can take the man out of the bog, but you can't take the bog out of the man'. His origins were also to be seen in the love he had for animals, especially horses. There was always a lump of sugar in the pocket, and if ever out driving in the country he would invariably stop if there was a horse in a field. The animal would soon sense a friend and come over to be rewarded with the ever-present lump. A nursing home in the parish had a particularly fierce Alsatian, or so it behaved towards Canon Nowlan and myself. But no such problems for John. The dog acted towards him like a long lost friend. He had a fund of stories, usually based on the three great interests in his life, the army, the telephone service and the Boys' Brigade. Each time he preached, a lengthy story was included. On one occasion a divinity professor in the congregation chided him for the regularity with which he included a story in his sermons, to which John retorted: 'At least they remember my stories – what about your sermons?'

He was a bundle of energy. As Canon Nowlan used to say, 'John would make you tired just looking at him'. But he was also a man of ideas with a determination to see them through. Three examples will suffice:

Under him a parish newsletter (*News for You*) was inaugurated at a time when such publications were not as commonplace as today – nor were there the electronic aids available that magazine producers have now. John badgered various organisations for material, acquired a second-hand copier, gathered a team of typists, assemblers and deliverers, and with great regularity the parish was kept informed of its own diverse doings.

The second example is the Kerry bus. During this period a group of Kerry pilgrims travelled each year to Downpatrick for the St Patrick's Day celebrations. It's a long way from Tralee to the reputed burial place in Co. Down of our patron saint. An SOS went out for a feeding point in Dublin. Just the challenge for our John. Another work party was organised, only this time it was a question of stew, mashed potatoes and custard. That training in the army and the B.B. camp was put to good effect, and many southern pilgrims went on their way, refreshed with a renewed insight into the fellowship of the Church.

The final example is the most notable of all. 1963 was observed as Columban Year, celebrating the 1,400th anniversary of St Columba's departure to Iona. In addition to the curragh rowed by twelve oarsmen retracing the journey of the saint, it was also decided to charter a ship to go on pilgrimage to the island. Bishop Tyndall of Derry was deeply involved in the arrangements for the sailing of the *Devonia* . But how to persuade enough people to travel? That was the question. Once again, it was John to the rescue when there was doubt as to the viability of the project. At the general synod that year he sat at a table in the foyer of the old Synod Hall, and at the end of proceedings had persuaded enough people to travel to ensure the success of the venture. It was a challenge he relished.

Such were the practical projects in which John delighted. He had particular gifts which he offered to the glory of God, and those gifts were used in a very wonderful way. It was to the credit of Canon Nowlan that he gave John his head, and to the parishioners that they responded in a variety of ways to his infectious enthusiasm. Later, when he left Rathfarnham, he served as rector in Edenderry. If there are animals in heaven they will have found a new friend with the arrival of J.J. – a most remarkable character.

In 1961 four regional press officers were appointed in Dublin, Cork, Belfast and Derry. They were respectively, the Rev. Guy L'Estrange, Mr J.L.B. Deane, the Rev. Billy Macourt and the Rev. Cecil Bradley. Their appointment was an indication that the Church of Ireland was beginning to think seriously about its relationship with the media. Up to this, apart from the list of Sunday services in *The Irish Times*, the only regular feature was the Tuesday Church of Ireland notes in the same newspaper whose inaugural contributor was Professor R.R. Hartford. Nor must one forget the *Church of Ireland Gazette* and its editor, Canon F.A.G. Willis, who was held in the highest esteem by the journalistic profession, and whose leading articles were acknowledged as models of their type.

In his presidential address at the 1960 general synod, Archbishop McCann alluded to the relationship between the Church and the media. In the context of the Decade of Evangelism his words were prophetic – 'In the sphere of evangelism there is urgent need that we should direct our attention to the use of the press, radio and television.' Over the years much has been done to improve the professionalism of those contributing to radio and television. Groups have been involved in training courses both in England and Ireland. A television studio is available at the Theological College, and those in training for the ministry have for some years had the benefit of this facility. Yet, despite all this, the question is currently being asked if in terms of evangelism we are directing our energies (and money) to the most relevant areas. If evangelism is proclamation, should we not be concentrating our limited resources on assisting those who write what many read and speak where many listen? For example, it was reckoned recently that 60,000 listeners tune in to the Sunday morning service on radio.

During my time in Rathfarnham I was appointed to take the place of Guy L'Estrange who left St Patrick's Cathedral to take up a post in Canterbury Cathedral. The position of press officer was part-time and the *modus operandi* was very much a personal matter as was the case with the other three officers. We would all like to think that we had a part in laying the foundation for what is now a much more full-time professional operation. We tried to keep the media appraised of what was happening or going to happen in the life of the Church of Ireland. The golden rule that soon became apparent was never to let an enquiring reporter go away empty-handed. The media responded to the efforts the Church was making, and gradually ecclesiastical news began to attain a higher profile, so that today the pendulum has swung completely in the opposite direction and Church news very often dominates the headlines. This is one of the areas where life has changed utterly and the Church is constantly struggling to respond to the insatiable demands of the media.

One of the pleasures of being the press officer in Dublin was the opportunity to rub shoulders with a number of outstanding journalists and, in a small way, be a part of their distinctive world. Those initially associated with religious journalism were people such as Kevin O'Kelly, John Horgan, Tom McCaughran, Joe Power and T.P. O'Mahony. In order to facilitate them and many others, certain innovations were necessary at the general synod. A pre-synod press conference was introduced; major speeches were made available before delivery; a press gallery was introduced in the old Synod Hall by commandeering the distinguished visitors' gallery (mostly bishops' wives!); extra telephones were installed; interviews were arranged. All of this may sound mundane and commonplace today, but in the Church of Ireland of the early 1960s it was well nigh revolutionary, and viewed with grave unease by some of the more conservative synod members.

From a professional point of view, it was fascinating to observe the different styles of reporting, and nowhere was this more evident than in the reports of John Horgan and Tom McCaughran both of whom worked for *The Irish Times*. Horgan would sit and listen and absorb the scene. His report was an overview without undue emphasis on the actual speeches. McCaughran, on the other hand, was a master at weaving together the various speeches into a coherent unity. Both were masters of their craft but from totally different perspectives.

Occasionally there was a hiccup as was inevitable. The most memorable was the year that the report of the Representative Church Body was to be introduced by Sir Cecil Stafford King Harman. His speech appeared in full in *The Irish Times* on the morning he was due to deliver it. The piece had been prepared in advance by the reporter with a strict embargo imposed. Alas, a sub-editor slipped up and the piece was printed a day too soon. However, Sir Cecil was equal to the occasion, and on rising to speak referred members to what had appeared that morning, with the comment that if the racing correspondent of the said paper was as accurate in forecasting winners as the religious correspondent, then the finances of the Church of Ireland could with confidence be entrusted to his care.

Sometimes an incident occurs in parochial life which has a far-reaching effect on the cleric involved. Such was the case one summer when Canon Nowlan was on a trip to America and I found myself in charge of the parish. A parishioner had been taken into a city hospital quite ill, and in the course of a visit she requested the laying on of hands. I was taken aback and, not being quite sure what to do, stalled and promised to return the following day. Normally I would have felt safe, knowing that Canon Nowlan would have coped, being deeply interested and involved in the ministry of healing. But he was 3,000 miles away. It so happened that I had met Canon Noel Waring in the rectory in Newtownards when he came to preach at St Mark's. He was the man responsible in large measure for the revival of the ministry of healing in the life of the Church of Ireland, and was highly regarded and respected for his work. What better person to contact? I phoned and asked if he would come and lay hands on a lady in hospital. My request was met with a firm 'no', and followed by a lecture on the role of the priest in the healing ministry. I was reminded that this should be a regular part of my priestly ministry. Fortified by this interview, I returned the following day to the hospital and, with prayer, laid hands on the lady concerned who eventually recovered.

Over the years I have found it to be an aspect of ministry that evokes strong conflicting responses. The devotees of the healing ministry are total in their commitment, often based on a personal experience. On the other hand, many are sceptical. Few would deny that there are difficulties to be faced – the confusion of healing and curing; the feelings of guilt where prayer does not appear to be answered in a specific way; the danger of the identification of this ministry with particular individuals. As chaplain to the national cancer hospital (St Luke's) for almost seventeen years I was deeply conscious of the dangers involved not just for the patients but also for their relatives, who at times were prepared to grasp at any straw. I sometimes wonder if, in the type of society existing today, we provide people with an adequate theology of death. We are bombarded with recipes for staying young. At a time of recession it is one of the growth industries. Yet, sometimes we forget that we live in an imperfect world. For the Christian the sting has been drawn from death. That is the glory of the resurrection. But there is still an inevitability present which is not always faced realistically.

One of the major developments within the life of the Church of Ireland in the early 1960s was the setting up of the Christian Stewardship department under its first director, the Rev. W.J. Arlow, in 1961. Today it is firmly established but initially its innovative approach was viewed with suspicion. It necessitated a virtual revolution in thinking and that is never easy in a traditional institution such as the Church. To appreciate the unease, one must go back a little in time to the late 1950s when a limited number of parishes introduced the Wells scheme of fund-raising. This was a very hard-nosed professional approach depending on the public announcement of certain financial pledges which were used as a lever to encourage others to follow. In other words, it used the inherent weakness in human nature to keep up with the Joneses.

In Rathfarnham a refined form of the system was devised, retaining what were regarded as the acceptable elements such as regular pledged giving, on which the parish could budget, and visitation of parishioners, but discarding the unattractive elements, in particular the public announcement of amounts pledged. The brains behind the scheme was Mr E.O. (Eddie) Foley, a retired business executive, and he was supported and encouraged by the rector who later became stewardship advisor for the diocese of Dublin.

There are still some parishes that baulk at the introduction of a stewardship programme. Certainly it is a challenging exercise, not just in terms of the administrative work involved but also in the manner in which it asks parishioners to think seriously about their Church commitment at every level and the use they are making of the gifts God has given them. One of the most telling comments made in this respect came from Bishop Arthur Butler. Speaking to the Stewardship Report at general synod when he was Bishop of Tuam, he said, 'Parishes should not ask, why should we have a stewardship campaign, but why should we not have one'. The introduction of a stewardship programme means extensive use of the laity, especially as visitors. As a Church, we have always prided ourselves on lay involvement, but for years it was limited to the administrative sphere, typified by membership of the select vestry. With the advent of stewardship, involvement was widened considerably by the introduction of parish visitors, and this has been the forerunner of various parish visitation schemes. Today we tend to take these for granted, and rightly so. But it was not always the case, and due gratitude must be expressed to those pioneers in the stewardship movement.

One aspect of Christian stewardship always fascinated me, and that was the different roles assigned to the female and male visitors. The ladies merely had the task of inviting parishioners to the stewardship supper, while the men had the more substantial task of explaining the system and dealing with any queries that might arise. When I enquired some years later as to the reason for this division of labour, I was told that it ensured the involvement of a group of men in the exercise, which might not otherwise have been achieved. I was not altogether convinced, as it seemed to suggest a secondary role for the women of the parish and perpetuate the myth of the tea-makers. And so, on the occasion of a stewardship programme in Zion parish, we introduced ladies as part of the main visiting team. They proved to be excellent ambassadors.

The early years of the 1960s were marked by a variety of events of significance in the life of the Church of Ireland.

Archbishop Gregg died on 2 May 1961, and shortly afterwards at the general synod, the Primate, Dr McCann, paid this tribute – 'It may well be that with the close of his earthly life's work, historians in time to come will mark the end of a period in the history of our Church'. In the same year Dean Lewis-Crosby died, having been ordained in 1892.

The end of one episcopal era was marked by the beginning of another when Robert Wyse-Jackson was the first bishop to be elected by the new electoral college system to serve the diocese of Limerick.

On the ecumenical scene, the British Council of Churches met in Dublin under the chairmanship of Geoffrey Fisher, Archbishop of Canterbury, while at another level the third assembly of the World Council of Churches met in November 1961 in New Delhi. Three aspects of the assembly can be noted: the presence of five Roman Catholic observers, the integration of the WCC and the International Missionary Council, and Michael Ramsey's speech in which he spoke of unity in holiness and truth. Ramsey's approach had the effect (and still has) of lifting the concept of unity out of the sphere of mere administrative expediency.

1961 also witnessed the production of a new translation of the New Testament – the *New English Bible*. Since then, the market has been flooded with versions and translations, often to the confusion of the public. This wide variety has contributed to a fall off in the memorising of biblical passages which was a feature of Church life not so very long ago. Educational theory also changed in the 1970s making such repetition unfashionable. While recognising that learning by rote can be a fruitless exercise if not accompanied by imaginative instruction, there is a danger that young people are being denied the opportunity of building up a spiritual reservoir which in later life may prove to be a source of strength.

During my time at Rathfarnham there developed a flourishing youth club of about sixty young people, many of whom were to distinguish themselves in later life in the professional and business worlds. Not many youth clubs can boast of a Supreme Court judge as a former member. One of the highlights each year was a summer weekend at the diocesan youth hostel in Strangford, Co. Down. In modern times weekends have become a regular feature of the youth scene, but then it was a very rare occurrence and may well have been the first such parochial venture.

On such occasions transport is always a problem, but we solved it by hiring a mini bus which was driven by one of our members, an eighteen-year-old son of a Monte Carlo rally driver! Even after this length of time I still break out hot and cold when I think of what might have happened – but it didn't.

There is nothing to mould a group together like a residential weekend. But it must be structured, and those participating must have a sense of responsibility, with a clearly defined programme and purpose on which to focus.

As we organised the first weekend I had the idea that we would call on my old parish of Newtownards on the way home on Sunday evening. There was a two-fold purpose – to beg some tea and also attend evening service. The tea, as expected, was a huge success. The people of St Mark's are given to hospitality. The service, on the other hand, was significant for another reason. Those who recall Northern Ireland in the 1950s and before will know that the best attended Sunday service was invariably in the evening. The morning was devoted to the lie in and the Sunday papers, but come the evening, everyone (or so it seemed) dressed up in their Sunday best and went to church. Certainly in St Mark's it was always a packed congregation with a wonderful sense of fellowship.

Alas, by the early 1960s, due to the advent of television, the evening service had been sadly reduced in numbers. My hope had been that the young people of Rathfarnham would experience something of the atmosphere I had enjoyed as a curate. But it was not to be. There was still a goodly number, but nothing to compare with five years before. The change of pattern was quite remarkable and left an indelible mark on me as we set out for home. Nor, I gather, was there a compensatory increase at morning service. It is a phenomenon with which we have been living ever since, and the drastic reduction in the number of regular evening services is a testimony to it. A whole breed of Church of Ireland members is growing up without experiencing the unhurried tranquillity of evening prayer. Few elements of our worship give me more comfort than the collects of Evening Prayer (BCP or APB) where we seek that peace which the world cannot give, and pray to be defended from all perils and dangers of the night.

If further proof was needed of the power of television, it was to be found in the decimation of Wednesday Lenten services when *The Forsythe Saga* was serialised on the same night at 8 o'clock a few years later.

While still a curate in St Catherine's I had been invited by Professor Richard Hartford to spend a year at Union Theological Seminary in New York as one of a group of twenty-five from different parts of the world and a variety of religious traditions. The only other Anglican was the Rev. Herbert Edmondson, a rector from Kingston, Jamaica, who later became Bishop of Jamaica. We were all part of a Programme of Advanced Religious Studies (PARS) and two years previously the Rev. Maurice Carey, later to be Dean of Cork, had been on the same course. It was funded by the Rockefeller Foundation with the aim of bringing together Church people from diverse backgrounds, believing that this experience of community would help forward the goal of unity.

This travelling commitment was carried with me to Rathfarnham, and in September 1959 I set out for New York, first spending a week at the Ecumenical Institute at Bossey outside Geneva by way of orientation. Attendance at Union Seminary for the year was to prove a watershed for a variety of reasons. The seminary itself was interdenominational, international in student body and staff, and integrated in terms of male and female. All these elements were far removed from the Divinity School in TCD at that time. The academic system of varied points per course was also new, as was the two-semester year. As PARS students we were expected to choose half of our points from the wide variety of courses on offer at the seminary in such disciplines as theology, the Bible and education, while the other half was made up of projects and papers specifically related to ecumenics.

However, the element that caused most surprise was the questioning attitude of the American students. Being the product of a system where to question a lecturer was to invite a reaction akin to that when Oliver asked for more – in other words, it was not done – the idea of someone questioning Reinhold Niebuhr or D.T. Niles was virtually unthinkable. Yet it was a regular feature of seminary life, and indeed was encouraged. To those attending third level institutions today, and not least for theological students, the seminar approach is common place, but thirty years ago it was just beginning to filter through to the divinity lecture halls of TCD.

The calibre of staff at Union was outstanding by any standards and in making up the required points there was an embarrassment of riches – Reinhold Niebuhr (in his last year), J.C. Bennett (Christianity and the Social Order), Kenneth Scott Latourette (Ecclesiastical History), Paul Scherer (Homiletics), Bishop Hans Lilje (Continental Theology) and D.T. Niles (Biblical Studies), to name but a few. For many at the time the greatness of Niebuhr was encapsulated in the famous piece of doggerel that linked him with another international scholar, C.H. Dodd: 'Thou shalt love the lord thy Dodd and thy Niebuhr as thyself!'

Courses were also available in such subjects as music, the arts and communications, which were a pointer to the type of church involvement that was eventually to be found in Ireland. But at the time it was almost too much to absorb, coming from a setting where liturgical flexibility was still a long way off. However, one could not be a part of such a scene for a year without imbibing something of the atmosphere, and in the years ahead I was to find myself reflecting on aspects of the varied experience at Union.

President of the seminary at the time was Henry P. Van Dusen, a former president of the World Council of Churches and a big man in every sense of the word. He had a vision of the Great Coming Church for which he worked unceasingly if at times, as it turned out, a little naïvely. Yet, if there is to be ecumenical progress, there must be enthusiasts who are prepared to be thought of as fools for Christ's sake.

It was a new experience to mingle with Van Dusen and other members of staff in the refectory. There was never a sense of them and us, and many a youthful idea was bounced off a world-famous theologian over a tuna fish on rye sandwich and a cup of coffee at lunch-time.

Not long after returning to Ireland, I learnt that Van Dusen had been involved in the ultimate dramatic gesture. He and his wife agreed a suicide pact and took their own lives. Apparently they had decided that their usefulness on the earth had come to an end, and rather true to character had made a headline exit. Because of his position as a leading church figure, the event caused a major stir. In basic Christian terms it ran totally counter to the traditional belief that one's life is held in trust from God and, therefore, its termination is in the hands of God. Furthermore, who is to decide when one's usefulness has come to an end? Some of the most inspirational people are those suffering from a form of disability which, in human terms, reduces their usefulness. In the circumstances surrounding the death of the Van Dusens it would even have been difficult to apply the phrase 'while the balance of the mind was disturbed', as their actions had all the marks of premeditated planning.

One other incident of a similar nature springs to mind, and it involved a rector in a parish in New Jersey where I was invited to give a series of Lenten mid-week addresses. One evening after the service, over a cup of coffee in the rectory, we fell to talking shop, as is often the case when clergy get together. It so happened that on this occasion the subject was preaching – its problems and opportunities. In the course of the discussion, the rector said that he always tried to preach each sermon as though it was his last opportunity to address the congregation. On the St Stephen's Day following my return to Ireland, that same rector was found in a lonely hotel room in New York, having committed suicide. It transpired that he was terminally ill, and this no doubt contributed to the post-Christmas tragedy. I often wonder what he preached about in that last sermon, and if, as we drank coffee the previous Lent and talked about preaching, he had some premonition of what was in store.

Being in New York for a year gave opportunities for worship in a variety of settings, ranging from high episcopal to Black Pentecostal. The usual routine was to attend Holy

Communion at 8 o'clock each Sunday morning in one of the side chapels of the Cathedral of St John the Divine, which was a short distance from the seminary. The cathedral is a massive building, but there was an intimacy in those early morning celebrations. It was particularly nostalgic when the service took place in the chapel dedicated to St Patrick.

Having attended the Eucharist in the cathedral, I felt free to wander and even sermon-taste. At times the wandering took me to such episcopal churches as Holy Trinity in Wall Street and the Little Church around the Corner. On other occasions it led to Riverside Church where Harry Emerson Fosdick had presided for many years, and to the downtown edifice where Norman Vincent Peale attracted large numbers with his distinctive type of self-help psychology. It's not without significance that Peale's book, *The Power of Positive Thinking*, is experiencing something of a revival in an age when the concept of the grace of God is foreign to many minds. As with Niebuhr, so with Peale there was a doggerel verse – perhaps unkind, but … 'Paul is appealing, and Peale is appalling'.

Occasionally I attended the Sunday morning service in the seminary chapel (James Chapel), especially if there was a well-known preacher. This was particularly true on one occasion when most of the student body crowded in to hear Paul Tillich who had retired from the staff the previous year. My abiding memory is of an eloquent preacher who succeeded in delivering a sermon without mentioning the divine name, which caused a deal of discussion after the service. Perhaps that was his intention!

Between the two semesters and during the Christmas break many of the students, including most of the PARS group, attended a World Student Christian Federation (WSCF) conference at Ohio State University in Athens, Ohio. Altogether there were about 4,000 present, and together with some others I was designated as a student advisor. This meant in essence providing a shoulder to cry on for any students who had problems. As most of the students were American, I am not sure how they reacted to Irish solutions for American problems.

The conference was basically an ecumenical exercise and,

in addition to a variety of seminars, there was a keynote speaker, Bishop Lesslie Newbigin. He spoke in a most challenging way, and not least on the evening before the closing Eucharist. He reminded all present that to receive Communion the following day was to commit oneself to work for unity. It was not just to be regarded as a passing gesture. Much has been written on the subject of inter-Communion. Is it the goal of ecumenical striving or is it a means to that goal? Certainly for those who on occasions use it in any sense as a means to an end, there must be a deep commitment to work for unity. Without that, the Church's highest act of worship is, in a sense, being debased.

One other happening at the conference is worthy of mention and that was a visit from Martin Luther King. He was scheduled to address those present in the main conference hall which was packed to capacity. I cannot recall the details of his speech which focused on the freedom of the individual, but I will never forget the sense of expectancy before his arrival, and the rapt attention when he spoke. One began to sense the power he wielded and the threat it posed to a certain section of American society at that time.

During the second semester we moved out quite a bit from the seminary. On Sundays I was invited to preach in a variety of churches in the New York area, mostly Episcopalian. There I encountered the unusual experience of being paid for preaching. This was a regular feature of American Church life, but at that time totally foreign to the Irish scene.

My most lucrative engagement was on a group visit to Washington on the Sunday after Easter. We had been allocated to various churches, and I found myself due to preach in the Church of the Epiphany. It was regarded as the diplomatic church in Washington, and on that morning part of the US Marine band was present to render suitable Easter music. Altogether an intimidating experience for an Irish curate. However, I did receive $100 for my effort which was the good news. The bad news was that we had all agreed to pool our takings to help pay for the trip. On the way home in the bus our director, Dr Ralph Hyslop, went around with the hat –$10 here, $20 there was the pattern. It was with some reluctance that I parted with my cheque.

My stay in New York coincided with the United Nations presidency of Mr F.H. Boland, and on the inevitable visit to UN Headquarters this ensured a certain one-upmanship. It was during this visit that a unique incident occurred. The young lady who acted as our guide was taken aback when, at each point of the tour, we were usually able to produce from our midst someone from the relevant country to which she referred. We eventually came to the trustee committee room where those countries who act as UN trustees for certain islands carry on their business. With a look of triumph in her eyes she pointed out that Australia acted as trustee for the island of Nauru. Little did she realise that we had in our group Itubwa Amram, a congregationalist minister and the first Nauruan ever to visit America. I can still see the look of disbelief as we trumped her ace!

I was in New York for St Patrick's Day, and like thousands of others found my way to Fifth Avenue to watch the traditional parade. It was a colourful affair as one would have expected. I was conscious that away from home the Irish, of whatever tradition, become very attached to the old sod. As I contemplated the cosmopolitan crowds and listened to the multi-lingual voices I felt like shouting out, 'But I come from Ireland!' Would anyone have believed me? A south of Ireland Protestant? During the year I discovered that for most Americans it was not part of the equation. Certainly at that time there was a clear perception of what it meant to be southern Irish, although I have never felt it to the same extent at home.

Later, a more sinister element appeared when I read an advertisement in a New York newspaper for a céilí to raise funds for those at home still fighting in the field. What a pity that in recent years the St Patrick's Day parade has developed similar overtones. There is a lot of work to be done if Ireland is to be perceived as a pluralist society, although the debate on the 1992 referenda indicated a greater sense of realism.

One of the features of Episcopal church life to take me by surprise was the number of clergy who had come into the American Episcopal Church's ministry from other traditions, or none. This was in contrast to the Church of Ireland where the majority of those in the ordained ministry have always had their roots in the same Church tradition, and in many cases come from clerical families. But it was not so in America, and the way it was described to me was that they had read their way into the Episcopal Church. This made for an interesting mixture because those who came from other traditions brought with them something of their roots, to the enrichment of their new found spiritual home. A typical example was Sam Wylie who had been brought up in the Presbyterian tradition before moving to the Episcopal Church (ECUSA). At the time I was told that up to 50 per cent of the ECUSA clergy had come from other traditions, and I believe that pattern has not changed.

Of the twenty-five who formed the PARS group, three were women – a Presbyterian theologian from Australia, a Church of Christ headmistress from Hong Kong, and a Baptist teacher from Sri Lanka (her sister was a nun in an enclosed Anglican order). Looking back, I am very conscious of the important roles played by these three ladies. Joan McNeill was undoubtedly one of the best theologically equipped members of the group and a strong leader. Ho Chung Chung from Hong Kong was a person of deep spirituality, and even today I can picture her leading our group worship by means of a quiet yet profound meditation on the Lord's Prayer. Ratna James from Sri Lanka had a delightful openness of personality and this, combined with a deeply personal faith, fitted her well for the role of guide, philosopher and friend, which she was to many of her fellow students.

She had never seen snow before coming to America, and on one of our class outings that winter, Ratna was found, in her sari and overcoat, rolling down a snow-covered hill. At that time the question of women's ordination was not on the agenda, but I have no doubt that thirty years later this positive experience of women's ministry was a factor in helping me come to a decision when this issue was voted on at the general synod.

One could not spend a year in such varied company without the occasional difficult situation arising. Two situations spring to mind which, in hindsight, were amusing. We basically occupied apartments for four people, with appropriate kitchen facilities, including a fridge (then a luxury in Ireland). My three companions were a Finnish Lutheran pastor, Maunu Sinnemaki, a Burmese Baptist professor, Tra Chit Maung, and a young South Korean Methodist minister involved in religious broadcasting, Jonathan Lee. Jonathan longed for some native cooking and proceeded to concoct the foulest smelling sauce imaginable, which he stored in the fridge. Christian charity can go so far, and after suitable negotiations it was agreed that he could only use the sauce after midnight when the other three members had gone to bed. I became very friendly with Jonathan, and it was an indication of the political climate at the time that when he contemplated making his home in the USA, I was grilled by two members of the FBI as to his movements in the seminary.

The other incident concerned my fellow Anglican, Herbert Edmondson, or 'Eddie' as he was affectionately known. Eddie was in the process of learning the violin. As a contribution to our evening worship he decided that he should join the pianist in accompanying our hymns. No doubt it was to the glory of God, but alas not to the edification of His Church. Finally, a deputation came to me as his co-religionist with the plea that I get Eddie to lay aside his violin at worship time. Somehow or other, I succeeded without causing an international incident, and took delight in claiming it as a victory for Anglican tolerance.

When the time came for us to leave Union Seminary, there were many sad farewells. Of the groups who had come over the years, ours was reckoned by the staff to be the most homogeneous. As we went our separate ways, we were conscious that many of us would never meet again in this world. Yet we were equally conscious of having been part of a deep fellowship for a year, which in a very real sense opened the ecumenical door just a little. In so far as our various disciplines would allow us, we had glimpsed the meaning of Our Lord's high-priestly prayer – 'that they all may be one'.

On the way home I had an opportunity to visit Jamaica for two weeks where Eddie was a rector in Kingston, the capital. I preached in his church, St Andrew's, at the main service which was at 7 o'clock in the morning, to avoid the heat. My host for the second week was a neighbouring rector who on the Sunday was laid low with a throat infection. As a result, I took all his services, including a baptism in a little church in the hills, Tom's River, where Basil le Roy Bloc was admitted into the fellowship of Christ's Church. I sometimes wonder what became of Basil and where his growth in the faith has led him. Such is the work of a priest that he often plants while others water.

While in Jamaica, I had an opportunity to participate in an ordination service in the Diocesan Cathedral at Spanish Town. It was a fascinating experience, especially when, at the laying on of hands, I discovered that mine was the only white hand.

From Jamaica I made my way to Canada, and eventually boarded the *Arcadia* in Montreal en route for Cobh. Before doing so I managed to fulfil a boyhood ambition to witness logs floating down the rapids. The sight lived up to expectations and I relived many an old movie of the early Northwest Frontier.

I also made contact with the Rev. Herbert O'Driscoll who had served as a curate in Monkstown, Dublin, before moving to Canada. He was always a noted orator and writer, and since those days has become one of the Church of Ireland's most distinguished sons. One of his recent trips to Ireland was to preach at the centenary of St Luke's church, Cork, where he was a parishioner in his youth.

The journey home was not uneventful. Because of an engine fault we spent two extra days at sea. As the passage was smooth it was counted as a bonus. At one point we sighted an iceberg which added to the general excitement. Apparently we were the first ship to take the northern route that summer, hence the proximity of icebergs. For the first and only time, I conducted ship's prayers, and was interested to discover the large number of people who attended.

After seven days we sighted the coast of Ireland which had the unexpected effect of filling me with nostalgia. Probably I was the only Irish person on board, the remainder were mostly American students, and so I was expected to point out the various landmarks. Would that I knew the coast of Co.

Cork as well then as I know it now.

As was customary in those days, the ocean-going liners berthed outside Cork harbour and were served by a ferry to Cobh. The *Arcadia* was no exception, and as the cathedral, perched majestically above the harbour, came into sight in the morning mist, there was a sense of genuine homecoming. What a contrast it must have been for those whose journey lay in the opposite direction with little or no prospect of return.

After the time spent in America, I was convinced of the value of adult religious education and the need to implement a programme at parish level. If this could be given an ecumenical dimension, then so much the better. With the full support of Canon Nowlan and an enthusiastic group of parishioners we set up a series of seminars involving representatives from the other main Christian traditions. We came up against one snag which, if nothing else, indicates how far we have come today. It was agreed that if we were to view ecumenism as something more than a pan-Protestant movement, especially in the south of Ireland, we should have a representative of the Roman Catholic church. We decided to invite Fr Michael Hurley who was then resident with the Jesuit community at Rathfarnham Castle. There was a negative response to our request, not we gathered at an individual level, but somewhere along the line the institution had said, 'no'.

How matters have changed in thirty years, and those who bemoan the slow rate of ecumenical progress would do well to remember such situations.

Meanwhile, in the Church of Ireland at large some important events were taking place.

In 1962 Henry Robert McAdoo, Dean of Cork, was elected Bishop of Ossory. In his general synod presidential address, Archbishop McCann referred to him as 'a theologian whose work is known beyond our shores and whose learning and gifts will be an accession of strength to the Irish Episcopate'. Not only was he to serve the Irish Church but, through his co-chairmanship of the Anglican Roman Catholic International Commission, for twelve years was to serve the Church Universal in a distinguished and painstaking manner.

Another subject touched on by Dr McCann was that of men for the ministry. He reflected the grave concern of the bishops for a situation which was accentuated by the number of younger clergy who had left to work in other parts of the Anglican Communion, and indicated that the signs were that in future years men of more mature years would be offering themselves for ordination. And how true this has proved to be. Archbishop McCann also paid a well deserved tribute to the work of lay readers and urged more use of the gifts of the laity.

In the same year (1962) plans were laid for the conversion of Fetherstonhaugh House, Rathgar, into the Church of Ireland Theological College, and this was formally dedicated on 17 February 1964. It has proved to be of inestimable value to the whole Church of Ireland as a residential conference centre with such ancillary facilities as the television studio and RCB library.

One final event in 1962 which is worthy of mention is the setting up of the Liturgical Advisory Committee. Since then the committee has served the Church of Ireland in a remarkable way. Our worship has been updated in a sensitive, yet realistic, manner. There has been a loyalty to the structure of Anglican liturgy, while at the same time a moderate flexibility has been introduced, together with a revision of language to comply with contemporary usage. It is akin to what Cranmer did in his day and generation, and in so far as one can say it, I believe he would approve what is now being done to provide forms of worship in the contemporary mode.

Occasionally a preacher uses a phrase which catches the imagination. Such was the case at the pre-general synod service in 1963 when Bishop Butler in his sermon used the phrase 'a confident minority' when referring to the Church of Ireland. It was a challenging thought for the Columban Year and it sent people out with a renewed sense of purpose. A couple of years later Bishop Butler used it as the theme for the keynote address at a West Glendalough youth conference in Blessington. It had the same positive effect on the young people of west Wicklow, many of whom came from parishes with relatively few young members. The core thesis was 'know your faith and don't be afraid to stand up for it by bringing it to bear on all aspects of life'.

At the general synod, Archbishop McCann addressed the problem of unemployment – 'Men and women cannot play their full part in life if their gifts are not used. The effects on the home and family are disastrous when there is unemployment and frustration.' Thirty years later these words have a tragic relevance and, unfortunately, are as true today as when uttered by Dr McCann.

Before the end of the year, the Church of Ireland mourned the passing of two of its most illustrious sons, Archbishop Barton and his son-in-law, Professor Richard Hartford. The latter was succeeded as Regis Professor of Divinity by Dr H.F. Woodhouse who had spent the previous ten years in Canada. Prior to that he had been rector of St Mark's, Newtownards, and a good friend of my wife's parents. Through their reminiscences I felt that I almost knew the future Regis Professor, and as it transpired, ten years later I was to have him as a parishioner.

~ 6 ~

The Garden of Ireland

IT IS AN indication of the lack of clerical movement in the Church of Ireland at that time that not until April 1964 did the offer of a parish come my way. As a result, I found myself heading for west Glendalough and the parish of Dunlavin with Hollywood Union. It was a delightful rural setting, and the contrast with Rathfarnham could not have been more pronounced. The excitement of moving to a parish was enhanced by the anticipation of marriage the following September.

The experience of being a rector for the first time brings with it a certain amount of apprehension. As a curate-assistant, one rarely has to make the final difficult decision. That is why there is always a risk when a parish appoints a former curate as its rector. It is invariably difficult for both parties to readjust.

As a curate-assistant, there is a sense of fellowship, and the weekly staff meeting can be a time of mutual support and sharing. All that goes when one is appointed to a parish without a curate. In that case one relies on the support of one's fellow clergy in the neighbourhood. For my own part, I was indebted to the wise counsel and friendship of my neighbour in Donoughmore and Donard, Canon Frazer. It was the beginning of a friendship and working relationship which has continued to the present day. We were later to become archdeacons, he of Glendalough and I of Dublin, serving under Archbishop McAdoo. And now, as Bishop of Cork, one of my most highly respected clergy is Archdeacon Frazer who, in his

retirement, serves as chaplain to Kingston College, Mitchels-
town, where his pastoral gifts and sensitivity are greatly appreciated.

One other source of fellowship was the clerical society
which is a feature of clerical life in many parts of the Church
of Ireland. The Kildare and West Glendalough Society was
strong and active and met on a regular basis, moving from
rectory to rectory. Apart from the spiritual and intellectual
stimulus 'The Clerical' was an opportunity to transact diocesan business and synchronise dates. At a time when there is
much emphasis on clerical stress, the role of these societies
cannot be overestimated.

Another cause of apprehension was the sense of geographical isolation. Although only 30 miles from Dublin, the
fact of having served in built-up areas for the previous eleven
years tended to exaggerate the distance element. Since arriving in Cork, I have come to regard 30 miles as a mere hop
down the road. But it was a real factor when first appointed to
Dunlavin, especially as the whole character of the countryside
seemed to alter when the Wicklow side of Crooksling Hill was
reached. This was particularly so when the snow fell as it did
in large quantities in west Wicklow. Indeed, later on, during
one particularly heavy snow fall, I had something of a pio-
neering experience when brought by tractor on a sick call to a
farm.

However, it is not without reason that Wicklow is called
the 'Garden of Ireland', and the seasonal changes in the
countryside were a joy to behold, not least when the sunlight
played tricks on Lugnaquilla.

Dunlavin is notable for the width of its streets, and the
Market House of cut granite which stands in the middle of the
road leading to Dublin. Loudly acclaimed by experts, this
historic building, dating from the early eighteenth century, is
known locally as St Paul's, for obvious architectural reasons,
and has been used for various purposes including a gallows,
fire station and courthouse. In the mid-1960s it was to be pre-
served as a national monument.

The town was also notable at that time for the number of
businesses owned by Church of Ireland parishioners. Most

parishioners were farmers, but during my time there were twenty-nine members of the parish living in the town – no mean proportion in rural Ireland.

The history of Christianity in Dunlavin is lost in the mists of Celtic twilight. Some maintain that Palladius, the forerunner of St Patrick, confronted the King of Leinster at Tournant Moat, a circular mound about one-and-a-half miles from the town which, according to tradition, was a royal residence of the princes of Leinster up to the fifth century. Whatever the accuracy of this surmise, the moat was a site fit for princes, looking down on seven counties and back at Lugnaquilla, rightly called the monarch of the Wicklow mountains.

In the tenth century, Dunlavin was associated with the Danes. *The Annals of the Four Masters* records a great fight that took place in the Vale of Glenmama in AD1000 between Brian Boru and the men of Munster, on the one hand, and the Danes and Leinstermen, on the other. All ancient writers place the Vale of Glenmama near Dunlavin on the road to Donard, and Professor G.T. Stokes in *Ireland and the Celtic Church* writes, 'the hostile armies joined battle at Glenmama, the Glen of the Gap, near the ancient but rather backward town of Dunlavin … I may just remark that no ancient Irish battlefield has been more completely identified and followed in all its details than this one.'

At the beginning of the thirteenth century the parish began an association with St Patrick's Cathedral, Dublin, which has lasted to the present day. In 1227, or possibly just before it, the then Archbishop of Dublin, Henry of London, created the Prebend of Dunlavin. This entitled the prebendary to revenues from the parish, which augmented his income as a canon from the chapter funds. One of the most illustrious prebendaries was Jonathan Swift. He occupied the stall from 1700 until 1713 when he was appointed Dean of St Patrick's. Dr Louis Landa in his book, *Swift and The Church of Ireland*, points out that to the parish of Dunlavin, then the name of his stall, Swift had no obligations. This small parish, situated on the borders of counties Dublin and Kildare, endowed the prebend with tithes – but not very munificently, since Swift's annual return was only a few pounds. The account book for

1708 shows the tithes set for £14. 8s. 0d.

After the disestablishment of the Church of Ireland in 1870 the connection of the canons with their prebendal parishes was severed, but the corresponding titles were retained.

Turning to the right at the top of Main Street, one sees the parish church. The ground on which the building stands was given by the Tynte family for ten shillings. This generous gesture is recorded in verse on the memorial to Eliza, daughter of Sir James Stratford Tynte, who died on 3 August 1816 'in the prime of youth'. The memorial poem runs to six verses, and verses three and four recall the gift of ground –

> *Dearest Eliza to thy memory dear*
> *This marble token of our loss we rear.*
> *This slab is spotless as thy generous mind*
> *But coldly represents thy worth refined.*
>
> *Thy actions will outlast this story's stone*
> *Thy gift the Lands on which this Sacred dome*
> *Erected stands this consecrated ground*
> *Devoted by thy zeal a church to found.*

The church is dedicated to St Nicholas, presumably Nicholas, Bishop of Myra in Lycia (S.W. Asia Minor) during the fourth century. Judging by the variety of those who claimed his patronage, he must have been an interesting character. There is even a prayer to St Nicholas, which, despite its doubtful theology, gives an insight into the variety of his followers –

> *Will you, Father Nicholas*
> *Sometimes pray for me?*
> *Will you give me too a place*
> *In your family?*
> *Boys and girls and sailormen*
> *And pawnbrokers are there:*
> *Will you, Father Nicholas*
> *Grant me too a share?*
> *Then, please God, you'll lead us all*
> *Up into His heavenly Hall.*

Altogether there are ten Church of Ireland churches dedicated to St Nicholas, but why Dunlavin came to be associated with him is hard to ascertain. Three theories have been propounded. The first suggests that Nicholas may simply have been the popular saint of the day when a Christian building was first erected in the area. The second hints at the influence of the Eastern Church on early Irish Christianity – there was a church of St Nicholas at Constantinople in the sixth century. The third argues that Dunlavin, being on the edge of the old Pale, and with such names as Thomas and Fenton still to be found there, a connection with Wales, where St Nicholas was popular, is signified. Local tradition said that St Nicholas appeared at a well at the foot of Tournant Hill where a pattern used to be held on the Sundays before and after 29 June (St Peter's Day), although the feast day of St Nicholas is 6 December.

As is the case in many rural parishes, the mix of parishioners was interesting. In addition to town and county, there were large and small farmers, those moving into the modern era and others rooted in a past age. Again, some identified with the local community while others stood firmly aloof. In other words, it was a microcosm of Church of Ireland attitudes, and an excellent place to have as one's first parish.

One other group was made up of Germans who had purchased property in Ireland. This certainly was a characteristic of Co. Wicklow, and in some cases it led to tension between the newcomers and the local inhabitants. Why they came to Ireland was not clear. It may have been simply to escape from the pressures of a highly industrialised society. In the parish we had three or four such families, and at no time was I aware of any problems.

The question of identification with the local community was not one which exercised my attention as a curate in Rathfarnham. To keep on top of the parish pastorally was a full-time job and left little time for extra-parochial activities. But in a country town the scene proved to be totally different, and not to be involved at the community level would have added considerably to the sense of isolation. In addition, as a group we can hardly lobby for a more pluralist society unless we are prepared to step out occasionally from behind the ecclesiastical ramparts. I reckon that in the mid-1960s there was still a reticence to be committed fully to the locality. Perhaps there was understandable reason for this in certain places. For the parishioners of Dunlavin, the harsh uncertainty of national affairs had been brought home by the tragic shooting of Robert Gilbert Dixon in his home at Milltown in 1921, and the vote of sympathy recorded in the minutes of the Easter vestry that year indicates the depth of feeling in the area.

Not long after arriving in the parish, I found myself caught up in an important community exercise – lobbying the County Council for a technical school. For some time the town had felt the need for this facility. As it stood, pupils had to travel to Baltinglass. For different reasons, I found myself on deputations to the Council offices in Wicklow and giving interviews to the national media. It was a new and exciting experience and was eventually crowned with success. I felt at the time that there was a genuine sense of appreciation that, as local rector, I was prepared to play my part at the community level, and ever since, I have advocated this approach. An interesting postscript to the episode is that, on a recent return visit to the parish, I discovered that the the new technical school now houses the Church of Ireland primary school, and an even newer technical school has been provided.

As is the case with any rural rector, I found myself on various committees with local politicians – pension committees and suchlike. It was then I discovered the encyclopaedic local knowledge possessed by such public representatives, and came to appreciate the workload they carry. In the intimate setting of a rural community there is a distinctive pressure on politicians which may not always be appreciated by those who live in the comparative anonymity of suburbia.

It was during my time in Dunlavin that the scheme for free secondary education was introduced by Donagh O'Malley. It held out the promise of an educational utopia, but from the Protestant point of view it initially fell a long way short of expectations, especially as a means test was introduced for grants that rarely covered the entire fee. Certainly, some in the parish looked forward to instant access to Protestant schools of their own choosing, and there was a great sense of disappointment when this did not materialise. Only later when five Protestant comprehensive schools were provided did the idea of free education in schools of their own ethos become a possibility for some of the Protestant community. Today, largely because of the burden of boarding fees but also in some cases out of choice, a significant number of Protestant children attend local secondary schools which, by their very nature, are Roman Catholic in ethos. However, it must be clearly stated that the school authorities make every effort to facilitate the religious education of the minority. For many a rector it is an ongoing problem how best to cope with the small numbers scattered throughout a school. The Board of Education has put much work into providing suitable material, and training days have been organised, but it is doubtful if there will ever be a complete answer to this problem.

In addition to the formal education of the young in rural Ireland there is also the question of creating a sense of belonging for those from scattered communities. One way of doing this is to bring people together for a central function. Two examples spring to mind:

Each year there was the West Glendalough Children's Festival. I soon discovered that it was eagerly anticipated by both children and parents alike. The event was hosted by a different parish annually, and consisted of a church service, sports and refreshments which were provided on the usual lavish scale associated with parochial functions.

The other event was a new venture which we entitled 'Teens and Twenties', and as the name indicates was geared for an older age group. On a monthly basis, a regular group of young people met together at different parochial locations to explore their faith and its relevance for their lives. They were already well served on the social level, and the parish dance was an integral part of rural Church life. But there was an obvious gap, and the joint innovation was designed to fill it.

Looking back, I believe it played a very useful part in stimulating an interest in the spiritual dimension to life, and the role of the Church in fostering that dimension. It was before liturgical revision came to occupy a high profile, and animated discussion took place on the need to update the Church services, especially the language. In fact, at that time this was a constant theme of discontent wherever Church people met, especially the young. The general mood, which was not peculiar to the Church of Ireland, lent urgency to the work of the Liturgical Advisory Committee. Our two prayer books may occasionally cause tension, but there is no doubt that there was a general longing for change.

The climax to the meetings of the Teens and Twenties was a youth conference held in Blessington and addressed by Bishop Butler. It was a memorable occasion with over 200 young people gathered from the parishes of west Glendalough. An American President once said that a person has never really lived until he/she has been part of something greater than themselves. There is no doubt that many young people went away that evening with a realisation that they were part of something greater than their own parish – the Church of Ireland. For some, that may appear as a narrow interpretation of belonging in the truly Christian sense, but with such a sense of identity there is less likelihood of becoming a spiritual vagabond. In this matter, I sometimes think back to a meeting for clergy in Belfast addressed by Canon Bryan Green, the well-known evangelist of another era. Asked (as could only happen in Belfast!) if he would prefer to be known as a Christian or an Anglican, he replied, 'First a Christian and secondly an Anglican, but it would be a very close second'.

Those meetings in west Glendalough highlighted one of the problems facing the Church in rural Ireland – the exodus of youth and how to cater for those remaining. It is a problem facing all Churches, not least the Roman Catholic Church, as I have discovered since coming to Cork.

An incident that occurred a couple of years ago will illustrate the point. I was travelling to a morning service in a west Cork parish and gave a lift to a young man outside Clonakilty. He was employed in a local hotel and was returning to his home near Skibbereen. In the course of conversation it emerged that he was the only boy of his secondary school class still in Ireland. It highlighted in a graphic way a perpetual problem.

'All work and no play' applies to clergy as much as anyone else, and while still in Rathfarnham I began to play golf in the local club and was given a handicap of 18. On moving to Dunlavin, I applied to join Baltinglass Golf Club. I filled in the necessary forms and waited election. One evening, a knock came to the door. It was the secretary of the golf club. He had come to make one or two enquiries about my application. The problem was the 18 handicap. In the area were a number of priests who regularly came home from the mission field, sporting 18 handicaps. Invariably, they cleaned up in all the local competitions. It was thought a little suspicious that a cleric from Dublin should arrive with a similar handicap. I assured him that it was genuine, and results soon proved the truth of my assertion!

One of the characteristics of Irish life outside Dublin is the provincial newspaper which usually appears on a weekly basis. It carries all the local news and gossip and acts as a vital means of communication within the community. In Newtownards it was *The Newtownards Chronicle* which covered the Ards Peninsula and was more than generous in its reporting of events in St Mark's. Every year it carried in full the rector's address to the Easter vestry.

In Dunlavin the provincial paper was *The Nationalist and Leinster Leader*. The reporter serving the paper in our area was Mary Norton, known to many radio listeners as Monica Carr. Each week she phoned or called for the local Church news, and one came to appreciate the valuable medium the paper was in keeping the profile of the Church of Ireland before the public at large. Mary became a good friend of the family and has remained so ever since, and when the National Ploughing Championships were held in 1992 near Cork, certain farming eyes widened when they witnessed the Church of Ireland Bishop being warmly embraced by the radio voice of rural Ireland.

As a Church we are constantly being urged to communicate our message. Very often the means of communication are on our own doorstep if we will only use them. So often it is a matter of building up a good working relationship and taking the trouble to provide the material, rather than engaging in negative criticism when events are not reported as we would wish.

Today, a further vital means of communication has opened up through the advent of local radio. The same criteria apply here, and happily there are a number of examples where Church people are playing an active part. As with provincial papers, local radio plays a vital role in the network of communications within rural Ireland. Granted, some people have a flair for this type of ministry (and it is a real ministry), but in the modern technological and electronic age it behoves us all to make the effort to respond rather than look on those who do participate as having succumbed to the personality cult syndrome.

Apart from the independent local radio stations, RTE has always been generous in its allocation of time to the Protestant Churches, particularly in terms of Sunday services both on radio and television. In general, the Churches have responded in a positive manner by the provision of training for those who participate, and the care taken in the compilation of the services themselves. In this respect, the Church of Ireland owes much to Canon Osborne Barr, who for many years acted as co-ordinator of Protestant programmes at RTE, and was held in the highest regard by the station. Another person to whom the Church owes much is the Very Rev. Maurice Carey, who was responsible for organising numerous radio and television training courses. Dean Carey together with Dr Kenneth Milne are currently the Church of Ireland representatives on the Irish Church Council for Television and Radio Affairs (ICCTRA). That there is such a joint committee speaks volumes of the place accorded to the Churches in the whole field of professional communications.

When the history of the Church of Ireland in the twentieth century comes to be written, the subject of parochial re-organisation will not be too far removed from centre stage. West Glendalough had experienced this when Hollywood Union was grouped with Dunlavin. By the time I arrived, the group had been well established and was functioning happily. Being a group meant that there were two select vestries. I have often heard it argued that this keeps the maximum number of people involved at the point of decision-making, and so helps to preserve harmony. Over against this must be set the additional work involved for the rector and, on balance, I would advocate a union where possible, with one select vestry. In our case there was the minimum of problems because of the general acceptance that the balance of strength lay at the Dunlavin end, where the rectory and school were situated. This had been recognised from the start and written into the diocesan assessment and parochial expenses.

The two churches in Hollywood Union were situated at Ballymore Eustace and Hollywood. St John's, Ballymore Eustace, was a delightful church, seating not more than a hundred, with a very fine high cross in the graveyard. The size of the church meant that the average Sunday congregation of about twenty did not get lost in a huge building.

It was there that I had my first experience of recorded church music. While undoubtedly a second best, it nonetheless provided a vehicle of participation in worship, without which the liturgy would have been very dead indeed. I soon discovered that there are two vital requisites when using recorded church music – a reliable operator and an acknowledgement of the speed of the music. We were fortunate in having a first-rate operator, Bobby Grattan, and I cannot recall an occasion when we had a hiccup. With regard to the speed of the music, I learnt my lesson the hard way at my first harvest thanksgiving service in the church. 'Come ye thankful people, come' was the opening hymn, and by the time the recorded choir had finished the first verse, the congregation was still only halfway through it. Ever after, on big occasions, I uttered dire warnings before announcing the hymns.

Those who visit St John's today will be aware of an impressive cross behind the Communion table. It was one of the first crosses in the diocese after permission was given by the general synod in 1964. The story behind it is interesting. It came from Rangeley in Maine (USA), where Dan Sullivan was rector. During my stay at Union Seminary, I had visited his church which was a temporary wooden building. In the process of time, a new church was built and the cross from the old church was replaced. Knowing that permission for the use of a

cross had just been granted in the Church of Ireland, Dan enquired if I could use it. The parishioners in Ballymore Eustace
warmly welcomed the idea and, after the due legal formalities,
the cross from Rangeley was put in place. In its own small
way it stands as a reminder of the worldwide nature of the
Anglican Communion, linking as it does the snow-capped
mountains of Maine with the rolling plains of Kildare.

It was at this time that the farming community launched a
series of protests against the Government, focused on the then
Minister for Agriculture, C.J. Haughey. As a result, a number
of leaders of the Irish Farmers' Association were jailed. A local
leader not included in that number was a Ballymore Eustace
parishioner, Cyril Booth. Cyril had come late to the farming
scene, and his enthusiasm bore all the marks of the convert.
His involvement in the politics of farming was total. I sometimes think of him when people bemoan the lack of Protestant
involvement in politics. Certainly we have always had very
few representatives at Dáil level, but to be elected to the
Oireachtas can often be determined by factors other than religious allegiance. However, in other areas notable contributions have been made by the minority community. In a sense
this is symbolised by Alan Gillis the current president of the
IFA. Certainly since becoming Bishop of Cork, I am aware of
this deep commitment on the part of many in the farming
community who see themselves as part of a large segment of
society which faces an uncertain future because of EC regulations. As it was once expressed to me – 'There is no such thing
as a Protestant cow.'

Being close to the plains of Kildare and the Curragh in
particular meant that horses played a large part in the life of
society. The national school in Dunlavin even claimed three
days holiday when there was racing at Punchestown because
of the danger from the extra traffic in the town. They also
claimed a week at the time of potato-picking. Such were the
idiosyncrasies of the educational system in rural Ireland at
that time. No doubt matters have been standardised by now to
comply with the computer programmers, but in so doing, certain communities may well have lost some localised links with
their past.

In Ballymore Eustace it wasn't just horses in general that mattered but one horse in particular, Quare Times, a former Grand National winner owned by Major and Mrs Wellman. By the time I arrived, the famous horse had been retired, but racing enthusiasts from many parts came to gaze at him simply grazing peacefully in the paddock. To have a meal in the dining-room was an experience, with the Grand National trophy in the centre of the table and the walls covered with blown-up photographs of Quare Times and Pat Taaffe at different stages of the world famous Aintree race.

The second church in Hollywood Union was St Kevin's, just outside Hollywood village at the entrance to the Wicklow mountains. It was claimed to be the oldest church in continuous use in Ireland and, being constructed largely of stone, this claim could well be justified. Recently I was fascinated to learn that it has been used for recording purposes by the popular vocal group, The Voice Squad, because of its excellent acoustics.

During my time as rector, there was a service each Sunday afternoon (except when snowdrifts dictated otherwise) with a small but loyal congregation of ten or twelve, headed by Mrs Gertrude Taylor who played the harmonium. I mention her because she typified the loyalty found in so many small rural Church of Ireland congregations. Her house near the church was also used for a regular Bible class. In hindsight, her contribution was invaluable, and at the present time, when there is such emphasis on using the gifts of the laity, I look back on the Mrs Taylors of this world and sometimes feel like asking, 'What's new?'

There was one other place of worship in the parish and that was Tynte Park School, which was held in affection by some older parishioners in the Dunlavin area. The Tynte family had been the big landowners for generations, but just before I arrived Miss Violet Tynte had died, and the Tynte Park estate was sold. The schoolhouse had obviously doubled up as church and school for those who worked on the estate, and in the mid-1960s it was still used as a place of worship. The agreement with Archbishop Simms when I went to the parish was that instead of a service each Sunday there should just be one on the first Sunday of the month. Although many people thought that services should have been stopped altogether (and truth to tell that was my own initial view because those who attended the schoolhouse were usually found in Dunlavin church on the other Sundays of the month), I was glad that a compromise was reached, and limited services continued. There were three reasons for this. In the first place, it provided a unique example of the division of the sexes in certain country areas at that time – the women all sat in the front and the men at the back, and to suggest otherwise was to be met by silent stares. In the second place, it provided me with an opportunity to play the hymns on a battered harmonium. My repertoire could easily be numbered on the fingers of one hand and so the congregation came to be very familiar with a limited number of hymns. I don't say they came to know them because nobody ever sang – perhaps my accompaniment left too much to be desired.

However, it was the third reason that really mattered in the long run. On the first Sunday of the month I had five services (including four preachings) in the parish, starting with 8.00a.m. Holy Communion in Dunlavin and ending with a 4.30p.m. Holy Communion in Tynte Park School. The schedule left me totally drained, and ever after I have been acutely aware of the problem of trying to fit in an undue number of services on a Sunday. This has become a real problem in the Church of Ireland as amalgamations have not always been matched by a corresponding reduction in the number of churches to be served, nor by a readjustment in the expectations of the laity. By and large, clergy are conscious of the quality of worship they seek to provide, but on many, an unreasonable burden has been placed. In my own diocese we humorously refer to the West Cork Rally Drivers, indicating the problem facing some clergy as they seek to cope with a time schedule which is too tight for comfort. A person cannot be expected to give of his or her best under such circumstances, nor can they hope to lead the congregation with vitality and enthusiasm if they are overloaded with services.

St Nicholas' Church was due to celebrate its 150th anniversary in 1968, and as part of the celebrations the parish had planned the redecoration of the church and the installation of a new central heating system. We had also planned to hold a parochial mission, and Canon E.M. Neill had agreed to act as missioner. Plans were well advanced on all fronts when, one evening at a rehearsal for the Kildare and Glendalough Choral Festival in Athy church, I was told that Archbishop Simms wanted me on the telephone in the rectory. I left the practice wondering why I had been tracked down at that time of the evening. My first thought was that I was required in my capacity as press officer. But not so, instead the Archbishop informed me that I had been nominated for the parish of Drumcondra and North Strand with St Barnabas.

The offer was totally unexpected. I was aware that there was a vacancy resulting from the sudden death in office of the Rev. Dudley Clarke, but the thought of returning to Dublin after just three-and-a-half years never entered my mind. My wife, Eileen, coming as a total stranger from Bangor in Northern of Ireland, had been warmly welcomed by all sections of the community (her mixed partner on the local badminton team was the C.C!) and our first daughter, Jane, was just over a year old. As a comparatively new rector, I was beginning to find my feet (or so I thought) and there were the plans for the anniversary of the church to be considered. All of this and much more was running in a confused fashion through my mind as I returned to the choir practice.

My wife sings alto and I am a would-be tenor, and so we were separated in the choir stalls. The look on my face must have said something, or it may have been the intuition peculiar to wives, but there was no doubt that Eileen was aware that I was harbouring some piece of important news. For others, as is invariably the case on such occasions, the hope was that I had not heard bad news.

After a period of agonising we decided to move and, on 21 July 1967, I was instituted to my new parish in North Strand Church or, as it is affectionately known locally, 'The Ivy Church'.

We left the Garden of Ireland with many regrets. One's first parish has special memories. I had inherited a sound base from my predecessor, Canon Cecil Stronge, and was fortunate in being able to build on it. The people were supportive and the mixture of the long-established and newer families seemed to gel in a way that is not always so. The pace of life was such that one could learn something of the rector's trade without feeling unduly pressurised. Today, with truncated curacies and bigger groupings, clergy often find themselves thrust into the midst of parish life without time to readjust.

On the wider Church scene the years 1964–7 were marked by some interesting developments.

The new Divinity Hostel at Braemor Park was dedicated, and later, referring to it at the general synod, Archbishop McCann said, 'We are confident that the changes already made, and those being proposed, will make for all round improvement in the training of men for our ministry'.

There was a call to take Advent 1964 as the beginning of a special Responsibility Year both to our own land and overseas. The Primate again brought a note of realism to the call when he said –

> Perhaps the evangelism should begin with ourselves. Do these our brethren for whom we are concerned see in us a better example of charity and kindness, simplicity of living and rejection of material values because of our Churchmanship? Do we present the image of a Christian Fellowship to them? Do we stand for moral principles and standards of behaviour in daily living that are distinctive?

In a Decade of Evangelism we do well to ponder these challenging words.

1964 will be remembered by many as the year when the bill was passed in general synod giving permission to have a cross in church, or to couch it in its legal terminology, 'to amend section 36 of Chapter IX of the Constitution'. It was proposed by Mr W.S. Milner J.P. and seconded by Mr J.L. Enright who later took Holy Orders. It provoked a lengthy and intense debate and, after formal statements from the assessor and president regarding the doctrinal position, was passed by an overwhelming majority of clergy (only 5 voted against) and a sizable majority of laity (Ayes: 102; Nos: 61).

1965 marked the end of SPAC's work, while in 1966 the House of Bishops issued a pastoral letter on the remarriage of divorced persons, in which an indissolubilist position was taken.

In the general synod of the same year, Archbishop McCann, in referring to liturgical reform, said, 'The Church must adopt this direct concrete kind of language if it is to make itself understood', while turning to the theme of ecumenism he said, 'Denominationalism is outmoded. Sectarianism is no longer relevant. The major issues of evangelisation in a secular and largely non-Christian world completely eclipse the relatively minor subjects debated by our forefathers.' Both observations were courageous and perceptive.

~ 7 ~

The Northside

THE PARISH OF Drumcondra and North Strand with St Barnabas covers a large area on the northside of Dublin from East Wall to the Drumcondra Road. On my appointment, I was heartened by one particular letter of good wishes. It came from a former rector, Bishop Charles Tyndall, who described his time there as the most satisfying period of his ministry.

Those who are interested in the parish and district can do no better than turn to the book, *From Age to Age,* by Arthur Garrett who was honorary secretary to the select vestry during my time as rector. It was written as a contribution to the celebrations marking the centenary of disestablishment in 1970, and contains a remarkable wealth of detail. A quotation from the book indicates the varied nature of the parish:

> Within the United Parish of Drumcondra, North Strand and St Barnabas there is a complete difference of environment between the area of each parish. Drumcondra may be described as a pleasant suburb of well planned housing estates and modern roads, whilst the North Strand is more a city parish, surrounded by roads lined with heavy traffic echoing all the noise of a busy, thriving metropolis. The parish of St Barnabas however, has an environment all of its own … a parish set in the heart of the Port of Dublin.

One of the differences I have discovered between Dublin and Cork is that in Dublin directions are given in relation to pubs, while in Cork the relevant landmark is more likely to be a grotto. Drumcondra church is a good example. The time honoured directive is: 'Take the Drumcondra Road and turn right at "The Cat and Cage".' There, tucked away in a delightful and tranquil setting, is the church dedicated to St John the Baptist, dating from 1743. It owes its origin to Mary Coghill who had it built in memory of her brother, Marmaduke. The interior of the church is dominated by a magnificent piece of sculpture depicting Sir Marmaduke sitting at a table dressed in the robes of Chancellor of the Exchequer. Arthur Garrett in his book records that the remainder of the Coghill family moved to Cork, and their descendants included Edith Somerville of Somerville and Ross fame.

Another interesting interior feature is the coat of arms of the City of Dublin on the south wall. It indicated where the Lord Mayor's pew was in the days when the first citizen and his councillors attended the church in state once a year, the Corporation being the custodians of the church. Shortly before my arrival, the church had been redecorated by voluntary labour and the coat of arms was resplendent with its new-found lustre.

Surrounding Drumcondra church is the graveyard which contains the remains of a number of famous people. One of the most notable was James Gandon, the architect responsible for the Custom House and the Four Courts. The Royal Institute of Architects erected a memorial to him in the church during their centenary year, 1939.

Other people of note interred include George Semple, the architect responsible for St Patrick's Hospital and the Blue Coat School, Thomas Furlong the poet, Francis Grose the antiquarian, and Patrick Heeney who wrote the music for 'Amhrán na bhFiann', 'The Soldier's Song'. We tend to think of the Irish national anthem in terms of Peadar Kearney who wrote the words, forgetting the other half of the combination. The two, in fact, collaborated in writing a number of songs. By all accounts, 'The Soldier's Song' was not popular at first, but it was published in 1912, the year after Patrick Heeney died of tuberculosis. Garrett makes the pointed comment, 'He was buried in Drumcondra in an unknown and unmarked grave.

He is unusual among patriots, in as much as he is unhonoured … but not unsung!'

In 1896, Drumcondra was united with North Strand. As the name suggests, much of this area had been reclaimed from the sea over the years. In 1786, Sunday and day schools had been established at North Strand Road, but it was not until 1838 that the present church was opened.

During the Second World War, in the early hours of Saturday, 31 May 1941, the North Strand suffered considerable damage from German bombers. Thirty-seven people were killed and eight injured. It was a sharp reminder of what might have been if Ireland had gone to war. Rector at the time was the Rev. Charles J. Tyndall, who later became Bishop of Derry and retired from the active ministry in 1969 just as the current troubles in Northern Ireland were beginning to gather momentum.

In 1965 the parish of St Barnabas was added to Drumcondra and North Strand. The parish church had been built in 1870 at a time when the parishioners numbered in the region of 2,000. But gradually the number diminished until the church was closed in 1965. One interesting sidelight is that in 1899 St Barnabas was adopted by Zion Parish, Rathgar, and each year up to £20 was sent to support the sustentation fund. The church was demolished in 1969, almost 100 years after it had been opened for worship. In a sense, it was symbolic of the demographic changes that were taking place, not just within the Protestant community but also within the inner city areas of Dublin, not least on the northside of the city. A classic example is St George's Parish where, as a student lay reader, I had helped to service its four churches. Not one is now used as a place of worship.

Two names are of particular interest in relation to St Barnabas' Parish. The first is Seán O'Casey who worshipped in the church and gained inspiration from the area. He gradually grew apart from the institutional Church but in his play *Red Roses for Me* he makes reference to a church named St Burnupus!

The second name is that of the Rev. D.H. Hall who served as rector in the period 1918–29. During his time he organised the St Barnabas' Housing Scheme, whereby people could purchase a house over a twenty-year period. In all, 176 houses were built. During my time as rector his was the name most frequently mentioned, and always with a sense of gratitude. Even the Corporation availed of his expertise as they embarked on the Marino Housing Scheme, one of the first such projects in the city. However, the real monument to this remarkable man is to be found in the houses of the East Wall area which gave security and a sense of independence to a group of people who could not otherwise have contemplated home ownership.

It was reckoned that in 1967 there were about 100 parishioners, many of them elderly, in the St Barnabas section of the parish. The closure of their church had led to an understandable sense of bereavement. It is not always easy to readjust in such circumstances, and part of my task was to assist with the process. Two factors helped considerably. In the first place, there was a sense of realism on the part of most of those involved and they realised that the inevitable had to happen. The most difficult period was while the church was still standing. It suffered from extensive vandalism and the fire brigade beat a regular path to its doors. When it was demolished, although that too was traumatic, it brought a certain sense of relief.

The second factor was the welcome afforded by the parishioners of North Strand, who grafted the newcomers into the life of the parish. And how vital this is in such circumstances. The two sets of parishioners had much in common and this helped the process. But still there was the need to extend the hand of fellowship, and this was readily done. By 1971, when I left the parish, I was not aware of any real dichotomy. One was conscious of the past and, I hope, sensitive to it, but by and large people did not dwell on it. A new spiritual unit was being forged and the future was what mattered.

The Dublin northsider has a character all his/her own. In relation to Church life it might best be summed up in the phrase 'direct sincerity', and this, coupled with a sense of loyalty to 'The northside', led to a deep involvement in parochial life. The men were never afraid to take off their coats when a

job had to be done (both churches were redecorated by voluntary labour), while the practical enthusiasm of the ladies was a
byword in the area. I began to realise the truth of Bishop Tyndall's words, and to experience the same sense of satisfaction.
Not only was there a readiness to deal with practical matters,
but there was a depth of spirituality which created a warm
and positive atmosphere at Sunday worship.

Characters abounded but two will not easily be forgotten.
The first was Miss Horner, who for forty years was principal
of the North Strand Infants' School. She had an intense loyalty
to North Dublin and to 'The Strand' in particular. Over the
years she had set many feet on the right path. She epitomised
all that was best in the national school system. Every pupil
counted in the most personal way and she was aware of their
home background, which often means so much in dealing
with children. Classroom facilities were much less attractive
than they are today, yet any shortcomings found compensa-
tion in the attitude of the teacher.

Miss Horner had one particular pet hobbyhorse, and that
was the removal of so many ecclesiastical and educational
institutions to the southside of the city. The catalogue was impressive – Divinity Hostel, Church House, RCB Library, Training College, Alexandra College, Wesley College, The High
School. She viewed this with alarm, especially as it placed a
heavy burden on the children of the northside. The provision
of Mount Temple comprehensive school went some way towards redressing the balance. In addition, she foresaw a
movement of the Protestant population away from the northside of Dublin, as parents sought to reside within reasonable
reach of the school of their choice. Later, when I too moved
across the Liffey to the southside, I began to appreciate the
truth of her comments, as the residents of the Churchtown
area included a good sprinkling of original northsiders.

The second character was Mrs Gray of St Barnabas' Gardens (one of the Rev. D.H. Hall's housing schemes). During
my time she reached the age of one hundred and was duly
honoured in the accustomed manner by the President. It so
happened that just after her birthday Archbishop Buchanan
(Dr Simms had been translated to Armagh in 1969) paid a visit

to the parish and, on hearing of Mrs Gray's milestone, asked to visit her. She lived with her daughter and one can imagine the surprise when at about 10.30 one evening the door was opened and who was standing there but the archbishop. We were brought in and found Mrs Gray sitting by the fire playing patience. Engrossed in the game, she continued playing. 'Do you know who this is?' asked her daughter.

'Of course I do,' replied her mother. 'It's the archbishop.'

Those who remember Alan Buchanan will appreciate how much he enjoyed the visit. As I watched I could see him back once again in St Mary's on the Crumlin Road, Belfast, in the 1940s and 1950s.

Shortly after arriving in the parish, I had the opportunity to appoint my first curate. On the advice of the principal of the Theological College, Canon John Brown I selected a young man just coming to the end of his training. Canon Brown had a justifiable reputation for being able to recommend the right man for a particular parish. It was not always the most obvious person but the canon had a priceless instinct for selection. Tom Moore came to a north Dublin parish from a farming background in Fermanagh, and turned out to be an excellent choice. There developed a mutual respect between curate and parishioners. For both parties there was the benefit of new insights acquired. So often those coming out of training seek a first curacy that will reinforce their own theological or political position. But the Church of Ireland is a diverse body and there can be mutual enrichment when these diverse elements are thrown together. What is required above all else is respect for sincerely held views.

The new curate had an excellent way with young people, and during his time in the parish a room in the North Strand school complex was completely refurbished and turned into a comfortable club room complete with coffee bar. The room was literally an annexe to the senior school, and so what better title to give the new venture than 'The Annexe Youth Club'? It was formally opened with a press photographer present. On the following Sunday a large photograph appeared on the front page of the *Sunday Independent*, showing Tom Moore jiving with one of the members. The caption read – 'The Swinging Curate'. It's said that all publicity is good publicity, and that photograph certainly put the club in the news. It was one of the first ventures into the club-room scene for youth. There was a recognition that very often young people just want to be together, without necessarily being organised – to have a place of their own where they can feel at home. The atmosphere created in The Annexe was an attempt to counteract the pressure of commercial interests.

During my time, North Strand church was seriously vandalised on two occasions, and a safe containing Communion silver stolen. Fortunately, most of the silver was recovered by the gardaí, but in a damaged condition. On the second occasion, the vandals used the building as a public toilet. The locking of our churches when not being used for public worship is lamented by many, but it is necessitated by the circumstances of the times in which we live, not to mention the requirement of insurance companies. At least one Roman Catholic church in the area had to remain closed throughout the day, which only served to underline the problem facing all the churches.

In 1971 a monetary revolution took place which was to have an unforeseen effect on Church finances. Decimal coinage was introduced. The old half-crown, which for many people had come to be the regular contribution to the plate collection, was no longer available. It was replaced by the ten-pence piece. The result was a reduction in income. This was soon to be compounded by the oil crisis which threw not just Church finances into confusion, but had a drastic effect on the whole economy. Parish budgets were thrown into disarray and it is to the credit of those in charge of Church finances at local, diocesan and central levels that the storm was weathered so successfully.

As ever, much was happening on the wider Church scene. *Holy Communion 1967* marked an important stage in the process of liturgical revision and was the experimental forerunner of our present *Alternative Prayer Book* service.

The report of the Advisory Committee on Administration, *Administration 1967*, took a comprehensive look at the overall life of the Church of Ireland, and in many ways proved to be one of the most significant reports produced this century.

Some words from the foreword give an insight into the thinking behind the report –

> If the society, in which we are called to live as Christians, has undergone great changes in structure and outlook, then the Church's ways of serving society demand the honest and searching review to which this report makes reference. In such a mood of receptiveness and readiness for action we wait upon the Holy Spirit for renewal of strength, with the prayer that He may give us an unfettered freedom to mount up and follow His guidance in all the truth.

The advisory committee consisted of the Archbishop of Dublin, Canon E.P.M. Elliott, Mr M.F.G. Dobbin, Mr V.G. Bridges and Mr R.C. Gibson. In the words of the resolution of general synod appointing the committee, their task was 'to examine the administration of the Church of Ireland as it is now arranged and to recommend such changes, reorganisation and reforms (if any) as it may consider advisable, having regard to the policy, priorities, direction and administration necessary if the Church is to have its full impact in modern society'.

Many of the recommendations contained in the report have been implemented, including the provision of nonstipendary clergy and the central monthly payment of clergy.

In his presidential address that year at the general synod, Dr McCann caught the flavour of the report when he said, 'To have a future is much more important than to have a past'.

While still press officer in 1968, I had the opportunity to be present at the launching of the encyclical letter of Pope Paul VI on the proper regulation of birth, *Humanae Vitae*. Apart from the content which reiterated the official Roman Catholic position on birth control, the occasion was interesting for two other reasons. In the first place, it illustrated a fascinating episcopal sidestep. Archbishop McQuaid welcomed those present and then departed, leaving Monsignor Cremin to introduce the document and answer any questions. In the second place, much of the discussion centred on the status of the encyclical, and how binding it was on the members of the Roman Catholic Church. I was left with the impression that it was pitched somewhere below a dogma but above a resolution of a Lambeth Conference, having the weight of the teaching office of the Church.

1968 was Lambeth Conference year which had as its theme 'The Renewal of the Church'. Speaking subsequent to the event, Archbishop McCann said that it

> ... laid emphasis on the gravity of the challenge to Christians in the worldwide problems of hunger, unemployment and injustice, as well as the tragic circumstances of war in different parts of the world. These are the major problems confronting us today. Our domestic issues are relatively unimportant when considered in this context.

In view of subsequent events, it should be noted that the ordination of women featured in five resolutions (34–38), and every national and regional Church or province was requested to give careful study to the question. When the pros and cons of women's ordination are being discussed it is important to remember that it was on the agenda of the Lambeth Conference twenty-five years ago, a fact not always acknowledged by those who plead for more time before decisions are made.

Other important events, both national and international, in 1968 were the commencement of tripartite talks between Presbyterian, Methodist and Church of Ireland representatives, a resolution at general synod to appoint a youth officer, the opening of the New University of Ulster with facilities for religious education and chaplaincy work, and the meeting of the World Council of Churches in Uppsala.

The year 1969 witnessed important episcopal changes. Dr James McCann retired after eleven years as Primate. He had led the Church of Ireland at a time described in other places as the Swinging Sixties. It certainly was a decade of much movement of thought and attitude, and a comment in his closing presidential address at synod pointed the way forward – 'We must become a changing Church to live in a changing world'.

Dr McCann was succeeded in Armagh by Archbishop Simms, and Bishop Alan Buchanan came from Clogher to Dublin. One of his final actions before coming to Dublin was to issue an open letter to the Rev. Ian Paisley, pleading for a peaceful attitude. It was typical of the man who, as an army chaplain, has been dropped into Aarnhem. At that time few could have foreseen the tragic situation that lay ahead and is still with us.

The new Archbishop of Dublin was the first chairman of the Role of the Church Committee, set up in 1969. The purpose of the committee is clearly stated in its own 1972 report: 'to encourage our Church to speak to the times and to bear Christian witness amid the tensions, civic, social and political, in which we live'. It has proved to be a vital vehicle of comment on the many ethical, social and political issues facing the Church and society today, and each year the report of the committee attracts widespread media coverage. Of its nature it cannot be instant comment, but its considered analysis is all the more valuable for that. The composition of the committee invariably reflects the comprehensive nature of the Church of Ireland, with membership drawn from varied political allegiances, community interests and professional backgrounds, in addition to the bishops and clergy involved.

Two important buildings were officially opened in 1969 – the Church of Ireland Theological College in March and Church of Ireland House in December. The opening of the latter marked an important stage in the updating of the administrative machinery of the Church of Ireland. 52 St Stephen's Green which had been the nerve centre of the Church for one hundred years, was no longer able to cope with the volume of administration. In many ways it was a sad but inevitable move. There was a homeliness about No. 52 which was distinctive. However, there was no loss of personal helpfulness in the transfer to Rathmines, and those who have to visit Church House today are assured of the same courtesy and attention.

Advent 1969 saw the introduction of a new baptismal service for a trial period. It marked another stage in liturgical revision and proved to be a most acceptable service.

The centenary of disestablishment was celebrated in 1970 with a number of events, including a Church conference in Belfast and a youth conference in Bray. At St Patrick's-tide an appeal was made for world development and world hunger.

Lord Soper was the preacher at the special pre-general synod service, and to mark the occasion a reception was given in the state apartments at Dublin Castle, hosted by the Minister for Finance and Mrs Colley. Mr J.L.B. Deane was elected a lay honorary secretary of the general synod and has occupied that position ever since. Indeed he is now the longest serving holder of that office. The new Representative Church Body library was opened at Braemor Park and, being in the grounds of the Theological College, is of enhanced value in terms of training candidates for the ministry. It now also houses a TV studio and video library. At the general synod it was agreed to set up a joint working group with the Methodist, Presbyterian and Roman Catholic Churches. In view of later developments it's not without significance that the first problem tackled was drug abuse.

Such was the variety of events affecting the Church of Ireland in 1970. In addition, no less than five new bishops were appointed: Richard Hanson (Clogher), Cuthbert Peacocke (Derry), George Quin (Down), John Duggan (Tuam) and Donald Caird (Limerick).

In his synod address, Archbishop Simms made reference to the 1966 *Instruction on Mixed Marriage*, and indicated that thinking was ongoing. This was borne out by the coming into force on 1 October of the *Motu Proprio* of Pope Paul VI. The Role of the Church Committee in its 1972 report commented that this represented some advance from the position of the 1966 *Instruction*, but Bishop McAdoo was more specific when he observed: 'The main stumbling block about mixed marriage has not really been removed until there is full recognition of the equal rights and freedom in conscience of the Anglican party'. Over the years this has been the crunch point which has never been fully addressed at an official level. Matters have improved considerably but there is often the feeling on the part of rectors that they are trying to obtain the best deal they can for their clients. If marriage is basically a sharing, then a legalistic approach, other than what is required by the state, seems very inappropriate.

A number of factors have worked to improve matters. There has been the ongoing work of the Association of Inter-

Church Families. And AICF, in addition to providing a support setting for inter-Church couples, has tried to ensure that the issue is firmly on the agendas of the Churches. On the occasions when I have directed couples to the association it has been very much to their benefit.

Another factor has been the pre-marriage preparation courses provided in some dioceses on an inter-Church basis. Again my experience of this has been very positive, and through them many couples have come to a deeper appreciation of each other's Church tradition.

However, perhaps the most significant factor in the equation has been the attitude of many modern young adults who are prepared to make up their own minds on this issue. An incident of a few years back will illustrate what I mean. For Church of Ireland clergy, attendance at an inter-Church marriage in a Roman Catholic church is conditional on the couple being free to decide on the future of their children. A parishioner was due to participate in such a ceremony, and the couple were anxious for me to take part. As I discussed the matter with the Roman Catholic priest involved, he said, 'You know, you don't tell young people what to do nowadays'.

One other incident in the field of inter-Church marriage is worth recording in so far as it gave me an insight which may well be unique for a Church of Ireland clergyman. While still on the northside I was involved in an inter-Church marriage which unfortunately came to grief after some years. The question of a Roman Catholic Church annulment arose and I was asked if I would appear before the annulment tribunal. I agreed and it turned out to be an informative and intimidating experience. Three clerical legal experts were involved and the questions and answers were tape recorded. What the ultimate outcome was I do not know, but one was left with the distinct impression that, contrary to popular opinion, annulments are not granted easily.

After the rush of ecclesiastical activity in 1970, celebrating the centenary of disestablishment, many people hoped that 1971 would prove less active. Such proved to be the case although there were some important developments. For the first time, representatives from the Presbyterian and Methodist

Churches were present at the general synod. This has now
been extended to include those Churches on the Irish Council
of Churches and the Roman Catholic Church. Archbishop
Simms made a plea for the work of the council, and urged
support. At the same general synod, fifteen bills were presented, which must constitute a record.

A full-time professional press officer was appointed for
the first time, and the Church was fortunate in obtaining the
services of Mr Charles Freer who had spent most of his journalistic career on the staff of BBC Northern Ireland. As one
highly respected in his profession, he set a standard which has
been very well maintained over the years, and not least by the
current holder of that post, Mrs Elizabeth Gibson Harries. Her
ability is held in the highest esteem throughout the Anglican
Communion as was very evident at the 1988 Lambeth Conference.

In relation to the wider Anglican family, the first meeting
of the Anglican Consultative Council (ACC) was held in
Kenya, and the two Irish delegates were Bishop John Armstrong and the Rt Hon. David Bleakley. The ACC has met
every three years since, and its members, both clerical and lay,
were invited to the 1988 Lambeth Conference. The venue for
its 1973 meeting was the Church of Ireland College of Education in Dublin, where the whole concept of Mutual Responsibility and Interdependence in the Body of Christ (MRI) was
expanded. Within the life of the Anglican Communion, which
is basically episcopal in character, there is some uncertainty as
to the role of the ACC. Just as with the Lambeth Conference, it
can exercise no legislative authority but it does provide a test-
ing ground for ideas in a comprehensive forum of bishops,
clergy and laity.

For me personally, 1971 was another year of decision. The
parish of Zion, Rathgar, had become vacant when Canon
Denis Hilliard, who had been rector for seventeen years, moved to Geashill. The idea of moving parish had not entered my
head, but in the early autumn I was approached by the parochial nominators. After consultation with the archbishop, I
allowed my name to go forward to the board of nomination,
and was duly appointed to the parish. The institution was

fixed for 24 November.

As so often happens in such cases, the decision to move was accompanied by qualms of conscience, often underlined by the many complimentary references to Zion in both the Bible and the hymn book. Each Sunday after my departure was announced, a glowing reference to Zion seemed to appear in the liturgical readings – not only was it a place to be sought after, but it was under the special protection of the Almighty!

My stay in Drumcondra, North Strand and St Barnabas had been comparatively short, just four-and-a-half years, and now, like so many others, here was I heading for the southside – the fleshpots of the southside, some even said! The parishioners had shown a warmth of affection to all the family, and my wife, Eileen, and our two daughters, Jane and Ruth (Ruth was born while we were in the parish), had put down roots and formed friendships. I was blessed with an excellent colleague, the Rev. Joe Perrott, who had come as curate from St George's parish when Tom Moore went north to St Columba's, Portadown. Joe later moved to Cork diocese and is, in fact, now one of my domestic chaplains. Added to all this was the thought of moving house just before Christmas.

But the die had been cast and I preached my final sermon in Drumcondra church on Sunday, 19 November, at a Boys' Brigade enrolment service. It was a great pleasure to be invited back to that delightful church earlier this year (1993) to preach at a Unity Week service as part of the 250th Anniversary celebrations.

~ 8 ~
Southside Revisited

ZION CHURCH WAS opened for public worship on 1 November 1861. To mark its centenary in 1961, a booklet of historical notes was produced by the rector, Canon Denis Hilliard, and Dr Percy Browne, whose father was present at the opening service and whose son, Dr Alan Browne, is still deeply involved in the life of the parish. This booklet gives an invaluable insight into the origins and subsequent development of the parish. It was amplified by a former curate, Canon R.E.B. White, to celebrate the 125th Anniversary in 1986. In an introductory chapter he sets the opening of Zion church within the wider framework of the life of the Church of Ireland at that period, and I am indebted to him for much of the historical material that follows.

To understand the early history of Zion church we must look back to the state of the Church of Ireland in the mid-nineteenth century and earlier. Before disestablishment the Church of Ireland enjoyed considerable privileges as the official state Church. However, there were disadvantages. For example, the Church's own parliament, Convocation, had fallen into disuse, leaving it no council of its own to direct its affairs, such as we have in the general synod. A parish was a secular as well as a religious entity. It took an order-in-council to divide one or to alter its boundaries. It was hard for the Church to respond to new needs, for example the housing development in such Dublin suburbs as Rathmines and Rathgar. To enable the Church to respond, a number of Acts of

Parliament were passed, encouraging the building of chapels-of-ease within existing parishes to serve new areas of population. A further extension of this policy was to allow a group of churchmen to provide for the building of a church in a newly developed area, without it being subject to the parish church and its rector, provided it was more than one mile from the parish church, and payment of the clergyman was ensured. Those who set up such churches were called trustees and the churches were called trustee churches, or proprietary chapels. It was in this way that Zion church came into being.

The other difficulty under which the Church suffered was spiritual. The eighteenth century had been a rational, cold-headed age which left a legacy upon the Church of dull formality. John and Charles Wesley and others reacted with an outburst of enthusiasm. This evangelical revival came to have two wings. One formed the origins of the Methodist Church, while the other remained inside the Established Church. It was these evangelicals who were ready and able to exploit the potential of the trustee churches, including Zion. Even the name 'Zion' strikes one as belonging to the tradition of Welsh Non-conformist chapels rather than the Church of Ireland.

The trustee congregations were among the most lively of their day. One of the leading clergy was John Gregg (grandfather of Archbishop J.A.F. Gregg) who later became Bishop of Cork and was largely responsible for the building of the present St Fin Barre's Cathedral.

Two people were central to the origin of Zion church. John Gold (or Gould) and the Rev. James Hewitt. Gold was a Dublin stockbroker, and a memorial tablet in the church records the endowment of the church –

In memory of John Gold Esq. of Cullenswood, Co. Dublin, who died 28th April 1855 aged 73 years. His desire in the disposal of his property was to provide a place in which the Worship of God should be conducted in simplicity and the Gospel of our Lord Jesus Christ faithfully preached.

The Rev. James Hewitt was the first minister of Zion church. Aged thirty-three in 1861, he came from within the evangelical tradition that had built Zion. Canon Bantry White points out:

> ... in Zion Hewitt faced no easy task. In an ordinary parish
> church, especially in those days, it might not be easy to measure
> success or failure. However, in a non-parochial Trustee church
> the Minister worked very much in the 'open market', where the
> success or failure of the venture depended largely on his pastor-
> al and organisational ability, his attractiveness, and above all, on
> his preaching. Furthermore, in Zion, Hewitt was starting in what
> nowadays we would call a 'green field site'. He would also have
> been more subject to his Trustees than a rector would be even to-
> day to his Select Vestry. The success of the venture is, in itself, a
> silent tribute to James Hewitt, who spent the rest of his ministry
> at Zion, until his death in 1895 at the age of 67.

It was not until 1885 that the rector of Rathfarnham consented
to assign a pastoral district to Zion church, enabling baptisms
to be administered and marriages to be solemnised in the
church. The geographical shape of the parish is unusual, long
and narrow, with the church just a few yards from the
boundary of Rathfarnham. This has resulted over the years in
a large number of technical 'accustomed members' for whom
the old marriage regulations regarding residence caused much
annoyance.

By 1971 six rectors had served the parish including Chancellor Louis Parkinson Hill (1919–50) to whose memory the
side chapel in the church is dedicated. He was followed by
Ernest George Daunt (1950–54) during whose comparatively
short term of office a broader sense of churchmanship was
introduced, including the regular daily offices. Ernest Daunt
later became Dean of Cork. Daunt was succeeded by Denis
Robert Coote Hilliard, father of the present Dean of Cloyne.
During his incumbency extensive building development took
place in the area and the parish expanded rapidly, including
the parish school which by 1966, with 246 pupils, was the
largest primary school in the south of Ireland.

In addition, a variety of institutions had moved into the
area, including the Church of Ireland Theological College,
while two hospitals, Mount Carmel and St Luke's (the national
cancer hospital) were expanding their services and requiring

regular pastoral attention.

Educational establishments were also on the move and in 1971 The High School changed from its ancient premises in Harcourt Street to Danum in Rathgar. Shortly after moving, it was joined by Diocesan School, which had found that the premises in Adelaide Road were no longer adequate for modern educational needs.

To complete the changing scene, the old Bethany Home (later the home of Mr Ralph Walker) on Orwell Road was developed as a hostel for the Girls' Friendly Society, but after a few years it was disposed of and adapted by its new owners as an extensive nursing home.

Such was the varied scenario that greeted me when I succeeded Denis Hilliard in 1971. His ministry had been one of remarkable vigour and the vision to cope with a rapidly developing parish. My first thought was – how did he survive for seventeen years in such a high pressure situation? Little did I anticipate at the time that my own tenure of office would be almost the same length.

In order to survive, it was essential to have a curate, and if possible one who could be treated as a colleague in the deepest sense of the term. I was blessed throughout my time as rector to have such men on the staff. In a variety of ways their contribution to the parish was immense, not least in the area of preaching.

To Cecil Bryan fell the lot of maintaining the parish during the vacancy, and introducing the new rector to its various facets. He was already committed to moving before I arrived, but I was fortunate in having him with me for the first two months. The prospect of a prolonged gap was not a pleasant one, but for five months I had Canon Cecil Proctor as an assistant, and his ability to readjust to the role of curate was a measure of the stature of the man. He lived at 18 Bushy Park Road, and in 1974 when he moved to a smaller residence the parish acquired his house as a rectory. The previous rectory had been at 5 Bushy Park Road.

In June 1972, Robin Bantry White was appointed curate, direct from the Theological College. As an historian of substance, with a gift for remembering detail, the background to the parish came to life in a fascinating way, and one was conscious of the truth of the saying, 'A people which forgets its history is like a man who has lost his memory'. He is now Canon of Cork and Ross and rector of Douglas Union, the most populous parish in the diocese.

Robin was followed by Patrick Carmody who also came from the Theological College. Unlike Robin who had begun theological training at the earliest possible age, Pat was a mature student. He was also a trained marriage counsellor and his perceptive insights added an important dimension to regular staff meetings. Pat is now vicar of the Christ Church group of churches in Dublin.

Next came Richard (Ricky) Rountree with the specific brief to put youth work in the parish on a firm footing. This he did by means of imaginative and hard work. Unlike his two predecessors, he had already served a curacy in Belfast before moving south. He left Zion in 1983 to become rector of Dalkey, and also serves as Decade of Evangelism organiser for the Diocese of Dublin.

Robin, Pat and Ricky all had one gift in common – they could keep the rector's car on the road. As one virtually devoid of all mechanical ability, it was a real plus (almost a necessity) to have a curate who could deal with the vagaries of the modern combustion engine.

Next in sequence came Marcus Losack. Marcus, an Englishman, had served a curacy in a tough housing area in Manchester before coming to Dublin to spend a year at the Irish School of Ecumenics. He was anxious to remain in Ireland at the end of his course and eventually came to Zion as curate. As one who had, quite literally, rediscovered his faith in the deserts of the Middle East, he brought to the parish an unusual dimension. He was also unusual in that his knowledge of the Church of Ireland was minimal, and so he brought to staff meetings an objectivity that is not often found in a Church that boasts a distinctive family atmosphere. It is hard to be anonymous in the Church of Ireland!

It was totally in keeping with his character that when Marcus left Zion he took up a chaplaincy post in Libya and from there moved on to serve on the staff of St George's

College, Jerusalem. Marcus and his family are now back in Ireland in Newcastle in Glendalough Diocese.

My final appointment to the curacy of Zion was Dr Michael Jackson whose father is currently Archdeacon of Elphin and Ardagh. A brilliant classicist and authority on St Augustine, Michael also brought to his ministry a very practical pastoral dimension, and the fusing of these two elements made a unique contribution to parish life. To him fell the task of ministering to the parish during the vacancy occasioned by my appointment to Cork. This he did with distinction before taking up the prestigious post of chaplain to Christ College, Oxford.

I mention these colleagues specifically as an indication of the type of gifts that exist within the Church of Ireland. Sometimes it is assumed that because the majority of clergy come from the one theological college there is a lack of variety within the ministry. This has not been borne out from my own experience as a rector. There is, I believe, a rich diversity, and through the colleagues with whom I have worked, my own sense of spirituality has been broadened and enriched. What is required is a mutual recognition of gifts which may vary considerably. Where this recognition does not exist, there can easily develop a narrow party spirit which is foreign to the mind of Christ, and divides the people of God. Some words of Archbishop Simms uttered in 1972 are worth pondering over in this context – 'May our Church's business always be seen to be our Master's business'.

Coming to Zion parish at the close of 1971 coincided with a dramatic rise in the cost of living, caused largely by the oil crisis. It also coincided with Ireland's entry to the EEC, ratified when Mr Lynch signed the Treaty of Accession in January 1972. Prices went up, never to come down, and in the following years the cost of living index soared. The parochial budget for 1968 was £6,500, by 1986 it was £40,000. The parish report for 1972 referred to the deteriorating financial situation, but the challenge was met when in 1974 a 42 per cent increase in income was recorded. The laity of the parish had responded realistically as has been the case so often in the Church of Ireland, right from the time of disestablishment.

It was also in 1974 that the rectory moved from No. 5 to No. 18 Bushy Park Road, the former home of Canon W.C.G. Proctor. Although not a modern house, the move was symptomatic of the trend in the Church of providing more manageable houses for clergy and their families. Most of the large rectories have now been replaced, and as a result of recent legislation certain furnishings are the responsibility of the local select vestry. In addition, most parishes who have a curate also provide a house.

All of this contrasts with forty years ago, when less attention was paid to the standard of clerical accommodation. The statutory free residence for the rector was provided but, beyond that, little thought was given to the quality of the building. What now happens is a reflection of the general upgrading of accommodation throughout society.

While he is in a parish, the rectory is also the home for the rector and his family, and the balance between use by parish and family is a delicate one. Often those who suffer most are the children of the rectory whose home can be transformed into a parochial meeting place. Living over the shop is never easy. Above all else, it calls for sensitivity on the part of parishioners.

The free residence also raises the problem of retirement. In contrast to forty years ago, many clergy, with the prospect of earlier retirement resulting from enhanced pension benefits, are now making provision for housing. Indeed, the retired clergy in the Church of Ireland play a vital role in maintaining liturgical life, not least in vacant parishes.

1973 was observed in Dublin as a Diocesan Year of Renewal and each parish was requested to hold a special event. Zion responded by inviting the Bishop of Northern Michigan, the Rt Rev. Samuel Wylie, to conduct a week of renewal in the parish. It was a memorable occasion, and did much to prepare people for a future that was to witness the shaking of ecclesiastical foundations. It was a period when the whole attitude to authority was coming under the microscope, and the Church was included in this scrutiny. Student riots in American universities were being repeated on this side of the Atlantic, and youthful unrest was permeating through to Church life, resulting in confrontation, which in Zion ended in the closure of its youth club. Sam Wylie helped to give our local problems a global perspective.

At the national Church level, the problem of authority was addressed in a publication entitled *Directions – Theology of a changing Church*. This was a series of essays, largely from within the Church of Ireland, which were designed to make a contribution to current theological thinking at the centenary of disestablishment. Some specific headings give a flavour of the contents – 'The Holy Spirit, the authority of the Church and development of doctrine' (H.F. Woodhouse) and 'The contemporary search for authority in Christian ethics' (James Hartin).

The Anglican Consultative Council held its second meeting in Dublin in 1973. Of necessity, it was during the summer holidays, when the College of Education was available. Because of this, the impact on local Church life was minimal. However, it was notable for the proposals to expand the concept of Mutual Responsibility and Interdependence in the Body of Christ (MRI) which had been first mooted at the Toronto congress ten years earlier. Guidelines for partnership were set out, and the resolution commending these states:

> ... that this implementation will help to break the old pattern of some churches as giving and others as receiving churches, and that it will provide a means by which all churches will draw on others for spiritual help and insight, and not merely respond to those who have financial and personal needs.

As an island Church, it is important that we have links at the diocesan level, but we must be careful that these links do not become financially burdensome. International travel costs money. Nor must the benefits be limited to the few. It must be a two-way process and involve a broad spectrum of people if it is to have real benefit.

At the hub of the administrative life of the Church of Ireland is the Representative Church Body (RCB), and guiding that institution is the chief officer. One who had occupied that post with distinction for many years was Derrick Pratt who died in February 1973. He was succeeded that same year by

John Briggs whose whole career had been spent at the RCB.

The following year, by way of experiment, it was decided to hold the general synod from Thursday to Saturday, and members welcomed as visitors representatives from the Irish Council of Churches and the Roman Catholic Church. Happily, this has been a feature of the general synod ever since. Events at the synod, which included the first report of the Select Committee on the Remarriage of Divorced Persons, were overshadowed by extensive bombings in Dublin on the Friday. As a result, the following communication was sent to the chairman of the Dublin City Commissioners –

> The General Synod of the Church of Ireland currently meeting in Dublin, having heard of this evening's bomb outrages in this city expresses to the chairman of the City Commissioners and to the citizens of Dublin its sense of shock and offers its deep sympathy to the bereaved and injured.

The tragic event was lightened by the occasional flash of typical Dublin wit. For example, the story is told of the spinster lady who was injured and, finding herself in the Rotunda Hospital, thought that all her wishes had been fulfilled!

Founded by Wellesley Bailey from Abbeyleix, the Leprosy Mission celebrated its centenary in 1974. It was appropriate that its president should have been Archbishop Simms. The mission has always appealed as an example of practical Christian outreach, and over the years its deputation secretaries have made a notable impact on Church life, not least in the schools.

In September 1974 an international consultation on mixed marriages took place at Milltown Park with a follow-up at Killeshandra in 1975. Having attended the two meetings, my memory is largely one of sadness. At Milltown Park we shared the Holy Communion in what was a very moving ceremony. Without denying our own identity, we were acknowledging that there is much we hold in common. Yet at Killeshandra one year later there was to be no sharing.

However, it is at such conferences that friendships are made across the religious divide, and at Killeshandra I was

fortunate to meet Fr Finnian Power from Mellifont Abbey in
Co. Louth. To stroll with him along some of the country roads
near the town was to experience a botanical treat as he talked
with authority on the many wild flowers by the wayside. It
indicated a lifetime of study and observation of the wild flowers that abound beside the roads and lanes of Ireland. Subsequently over the years it was a great joy to visit the abbey and,
with my wife, to enjoy the hospitality which is such a feature
of community life.

After lengthy discussion, 1975 saw the introduction of
boards of management for primary schools. These replaced
the old system of clerical manager, although in many cases the
local clergyman remained as chairman of the board. One
notable exception was the Diocese of Cork, Cloyne and Ross
where the majority of chairmen are lay. The new system involved both teachers and parents, and so gave direct involvement in the management of schools to two concerned groups.

One small landmark to note in 1975 was the centenary of
the general synod in the Synod Hall. It was held there until
1983 when it moved to the Royal Dublin Society in Balls-
bridge. Two years later, in 1985, the synod met for the first
time outside Dublin, in the City Hall, Belfast.

At the 1975 pre-synod service Bishop Quin of Down and
Dromore reminded the congregation of the troubles still af-
flicting Northern Irish society, and pointed the way forward
when he said, 'The evil all around us must be overcome with
good'. After almost twenty-five years of conflict, there are
many who cast doubt on the ability of the Church to contri-
bute to a solution. Yet, without the reconciling influence of the
Churches during that period, matters would surely be much
worse.

At the synod an in-depth report was produced by the
committee dealing with the remarriage of divorced persons in
church. That the synod is still grappling with this issue is an
indication of its complexity and the feeling it is likely to en-
gender. The synod was also reminded of an instruction from
the bishops on mixed marriage which was quoted in the report of the Role of the Church Committee.

The instruction stressed the need for consultation, and

there is no doubt that this now takes place to a much greater extent than heretofore. In the same report, four lines appeared under the heading 'Feakle'. The brief comment was as follows:

> The Committee respects the courage and integrity of those churchmen, clerical and lay, who, acting on their own responsibility, engaged in the meeting at Feakle and subsequent contacts with Provisional Sinn Féin.

At the time it caused quite a stir, but it did result in a brief lull in hostilities. The tragedy is that now, almost twenty-five years on, the courage and integrity referred to in the report appear to have been in vain.

Meanwhile, the global ecumenists continued on their travels, and the fifth assembly of the World Council of Churches was held in Nairobi. At home, an event of some significance took place in Armagh Cathedral on St Columba's Day when Dr Robin Eames was consecrated bishop at the age of thirty-eight, to serve in the United Dioceses of Derry and Raphoe.

Today we have come to take for granted the presence of lady lay readers. However, in the mid-1970s they had not yet made their appearance. Archbishop Buchanan in Dublin obviously felt this to be a lack and he approached five ladies with a view to training them to be commissioned in the diocese. One was a Zion parishioner, Mrs Thea Boyle, whose father had been a rector in Clogher. After a year's intensive training by the archbishop himself, the five ladies were commissioned on 16 November 1975. In many ways it was a milestone in the life of the Church of Ireland, and those who had the privilege of working with the five readers soon came to appreciate their worth. As with the three ladies in the seminary in New York fifteen years earlier, this experience further commended to me the ministry of women in the Church. In view of the archbishop's direct involvement, it came as no surprise the following year when he proposed a motion at the general synod, seconded by the Bishop of Kilmore, that was to reach a climax fifteen years later in the vote to permit the ordination of women to the priesthood. The original motion ran as follows –

That this house approves in principle the ordination of women, subject to the enactment of any necessary legislation, and requests that a copy of this resolution be sent to the Secretary General of the Anglican Consultative Council.

Apart from the archbishop's motion, the general synod of 1976 was notable for at least two other events. One was the introduction of a bill to establish the Church of Ireland Pensions' Fund which, in the intervening years, has developed to the extent that clergy can now retire on full pension at sixty-eight. During the previous year, 1975, clergy had been admitted to the state pension scheme for the first time. The second important event was the retirement, after twenty-one years service, of Archdeacon Jenkins as one of the honorary secretaries of the synod. He was replaced by Noel Willoughby, who was later to be elected Bishop of Cashel and Ossory.

One of the prime responsibilities of a rector is the worship of the parish. To exercise this responsibility while remaining true to the Anglican tradition of formal services is not always easy in the current flexible liturgical climate. In Zion, it resulted in the introduction of the first regular Folk Holy Communion in the Church of Ireland. This was in no small measure due to the organist, David Wilkinson, a man of immense enthusiasm, who had heard what was happening in this field within the Roman Catholic Church, especially in Rathmines. We visited the service and were impressed with what we saw and heard. Convinced that this was something we should attempt in our own setting, we gathered a group of young musicians and prepared for our first service. Underlining the whole project was the recognition that this was an act of worship, and therefore must be the best that we could offer, and those participating must be conscious of the example they were setting. The service became a regular feature of parish life once a month, and the group was invited to lead worship in churches throughout Ireland in the succeeding years. They even went on tour to England as well as taking part in a number of Sunday morning services from RTE.

In 1976, after careful consideration, Christian Stewardship was introduced into the parish. Like many other parishes, the

idea had at first been rejected, yet when it was inaugurated
parishioners began to experience a greater sense of involvement, and were regularly challenged in their attitude to
Church membership.

Stewardship is really an attitude of mind, and one unique
extension of the concept in Zion was the conversion of the
north transept and gallery of the church into commercial offices in 1984. This 'first' in the Church of Ireland has been the
cause of much favourable comment as an imaginative stewardship of unused space.

A number of factors combined to bring the project about.
The particular area was rarely used and it seemed a waste of
space. Various suggestions had been made including the provision of a 'friendly room' where people could drop in for a
chat and a cup of tea. Invariably, finance was the stumbling
block. Then a report on the fabric of the church indicated that
at least £100,000 would need to be spent over a period in order
to maintain the building, apart from any crisis that might arise
– and in Zion dry rot was a constant menace.

Why not put the unused space to work in order to gener-
ate income to maintain the rest of the building? The parish
was fortunate in having the right people to promote this idea
and see it through, and the committee that was formed consisted of some of the leading professional men in Dublin. The
parishioners almost unanimously embraced the idea and, once
the select vestry had given approval, the work began. It would
be hard to describe the dust, but we all survived that and
those looking at the church now, either inside or outside,
would find it difficult to pinpoint where the work had been
carried out. The symmetry on the outside is in no way damaged, and the interior is not only adequate but, in some ways,
is enhanced by removing a large open space.

At a time when many of our church buildings are under
scrutiny, it behoves us to use a little imagination. Every context is different but what is called for is vision, and a recognition that what was suitable for a past era may not be appropriate today.

There are a number of examples of imaginative use of
space. In Dublin, Donnybrook and Irishtown led the way by

partitioning the church building, while Rathmines is a further example of what can be achieved. In Cork, where there are a number of redundant churches, as a result of the recommendations of the Commission on Church Buildings, some parishes and communities have displayed commendable innovative sense in developing such projects as a stained glass museum, an education and retreat centre and a heritage centre. I believe that such projects should be given every encouragement both at diocesan and central Church level. Apart from their intrinsic value, such support helps to relieve the undoubted trauma experienced locally when a church is closed.

I mentioned the sexton who was in Rathfarnham when I went as a curate. In Zion, we had another character: Henry Murphy, or Mr Murphy as he was referred to by all and sundry. He had a great affection for the Church and the things of the Church. He never missed a daily service and always seemed to be there when wanted. When he died suddenly one Saturday morning (I heard of his death on the third green at Rathfarnham golf club), it left a void, not just in the life of the parish as a whole, but in the lives of many individuals, and especially the pupils of the school, for whom he had a particular affection. He was one of a passing breed of full-time sextons, and today many churches rely on voluntary workers.

Looking back on sixteen years in Zion Parish, many highlights stand out. In addition to those already mentioned, three others can be underlined – school, hospitals and ecumenical relations.

The primary school, dating from the same time as the church, was an integral part of parish life. Through all the changes of curriculum, teaching methods, management and staff, it retained its vibrancy. Because of the constraints of space, it had to double up with a variety of parochial organisations but, with few exceptions, peace prevailed. This was in no small measure due to the calibre of leadership both in school and parochial organisations. Involvement with a well-run school is a great joy and a real pastoral opportunity. Such was my experience in Zion.

The whole subject of education is in the melting pot at present. Those who clamour for change at the primary level do not always seem to appreciate the input of clergy down through the years. By the less charitable it is interpreted as part of an indoctrination process and an attempt to wield power at the tax-payers' expense. Certainly in the context of the Church of Ireland, I do not believe that that is so. Rather I see it as a response to the expressed wishes of the members of our Church who, for the most part, seek to have their children educated in schools reflecting their own religious ethos. The indications are that not too many Church of Ireland children are to be found in project schools.

The second highlight was the hospital work – time-consuming but very rewarding. There were two hospitals of contrasting style; Mount Carmel (general and maternity) and St Luke's (the national cancer hospital). In both hospitals the chaplains were regarded as vital cogs in the caring machine. It is one of the facts of Church of Ireland life that, in the vast majority of cases, hospital chaplaincy work goes with the parish. If there is a hospital, of whatever type, then the rector assumes the role of chaplain. In the majority of cases it works reasonably well, but there can be misfits, and when that happens the Church, not to mention the hospital, has a problem on its hands. People are at their most vulnerable when in hospital and the first essential for the chaplain is sensitivity. In the truest sense of the word he/she needs to be professional, especially as remuneration is now paid both by the Department of Health and many private hospitals. This is one of the changes that has taken place over the years.

In order to raise the standard, a number of chaplains have been sent to intensive summer courses in England, and in-service days are held in some dioceses, hosted by the hospital authorities. Developments in both medicine and counselling are ongoing, and the Church must equip its chaplains to keep up with the changes.

In the course of hospital work over the years, I discovered that one of the most comforting experiences for a patient was when I could relate to them through a mutual acquaintance. There is a great sense of isolation when going into hospital, especially for the first time. But if a point of contact can be made, it seems to lessen the isolation and create a bond.

The third factor I would highlight is ecumenical relations: shortly after arriving in the parish, the Ballymascanlon inter-Church talks commenced. There were great expectations. Following one meeting, I received a telephone call from Fr Gerry Reynolds, a Redemptorist priest stationed in Marianella Retreat House in Rathgar. He said that, as a result of what he had seen of the talks, he believed that unless there were local initiatives, ecumenical progress would be stifled. So he invited the local clergy to meet at Marianella – Roman Catholic, Presbyterian, Methodist and Church of Ireland. We met on a regular basis – about every six weeks – for prayer and discussion. Nothing elaborate was attempted. It was as though we were letting the Spirit lead us. When Fr Gerry was transferred, his place was taken by Fr Kevin Donlon, and the tradition carried on. Eventually we moved out and rotated amongst the various dwelling places. Through our meeting and sharing there grew up an atmosphere of mutual trust and respect which, I believe, is the only foundation for true ecumenism. In the deepest sense we could speak the truth in love, without fear of hurt.

However, ecumenism is not just a clerical prerogative, and so, under the guidance of the Rev. Patrick Semple, then adult education officer in the Church of Ireland, we set up a series of inter-Church lay groups. Each group was hand-picked and consisted of ten people. No agenda was set but the group, through open discussion, came to fix on the subjects it wanted to examine. These covered a whole range of potentially divisive issues of a theological and ethical nature. Once a year all the group members met with the clergy for a time of sharing, and, if necessary, clarification. It soon became obvious that the same sense of trust as existed in the clerical group was developing amongst the laity. During the week of prayer for unity it was the groups that organised the annual service. No longer was it merely a clerical event as is often the case.

Out of the whole ecumenical scene, and enhancing it, developed a community festival. It is not enough for people to pray together, they must play together. In this way, ecumenical relations are not just seen in terms of hothouse activities. The Terenure Festival owed its origin to the initiative of Fr Teddy Downes, one of the curates in St Joseph's, Terenure.

One morning he called to the rectory to float the idea, and he found a ready taker. As more or less self-appointed joint chairmen, we gathered together a committee and set about putting a week-long festival together. Starting out with no money but the hope of an Arts Council grant, we decided to pitch our sights high, in the belief that if the artists were of sufficient calibre, people would come. And so it turned out, but not before there was many a sleepless night. Every church and hall in the area was used, and they were well filled to hear such artists as John O'Connor, Frank Patterson, Eily O'Grady, Paul Brady, Jimmy Crowley, the No. 1 Army Band and many more. For three years we maintained the same high standard before deciding to have a break. It was a time of excitement, and the working together at what was a non-theological level enhanced the whole ecumenical atmosphere.

Since those days, I have never underestimated the value and influence of community events and have constantly urged people to get involved. Indeed, one of the features of rural Ireland is the growth of community festivals. If the happy results of a Dublin suburb are anything to go by, then they are well worth whatever hard work may be involved.

In 1977 Archbishop Buchanan retired from Dublin and was replaced by Dr McAdoo. During his time in Dublin, Dr Buchanan had displayed a great depth of pastoral care. On a personal level, I was deeply conscious of this. It so happened that our older daughter, then aged three, was in Crumlin hospital on the day of his enthronement in Christ Church Cathedral. After the ceremony, he insisted on being driven to the hospital to see her. Such actions are not soon forgotten, even by a three-year-old! Dr Simms caught the mood when he said of Archbishop Buchanan – 'He was never content with mere analysis, but longed where possible to give suggestions and leadings that were positive and constructive.'

Another important event in 1977 was the Partners in Mission Consultation held in September. Representatives from a number of overseas provinces came to Ireland and, together with delegates from each diocese, met to examine the life of the Church of Ireland. By all accounts, it was a period of deep heart-searching as our overseas partners drew attention to the

binding chains of history. Sometimes we need those from outside to give us a true picture of ourselves. A second consultation was held in 1983, but since then the concept seems to have
fallen into abeyance, at least as far as the Church of Ireland is
concerned. Could it be that we found the objective analysis of
our partners too difficult to absorb?

1978 was another Lambeth year under the chairmanship
of Archbishop Coggan, but before the Irish bishops left for the
conference they indicated that they saw no valid theological
objection to the ordination of women. This was one of the subjects addressed at Lambeth, and the conference encouraged
'all member Churches of the Anglican Communion to continue in communion with one another, notwithstanding the
admission of women (whether at present or in the future) to
the ordained ministry of some member Churches'. It also recognised the autonomy of each of its member Churches and
acknowledged the legal right of each Church to make its own
decision about the appropriateness of admitting women to
Holy Orders. There was also a recognition that such provincial
action would have 'consequences of the utmost significance
for the Anglican Communion as a whole'.

When the conference met in 1978, Canada, the United
States, New Zealand and the Diocese of Hong Kong had already admitted women to the priesthood. It was to be another
twelve years before the Church of Ireland took its historic
vote.

Another problem addressed, of particular relevance to
Ireland, was that of Anglican-Roman Catholic marriages. The
conference, while welcoming the report of the Anglican-
Roman Catholic Commission on *The Theology of Marriage and
its Application to Mixed Marriages* (1975), went on to point out
that the problems associated with marriage between members
of the two Communions continued to hinder inter-Church
relations and progress towards unity, especially as the general
principles underlying the Roman Catholic position were un-
acceptable to Anglicans.

A feature of Lambeth 1978 was the shift in balance of
membership. Archbishop McAdoo, addressing the Dublin
Synod that year, summed up the position when he said:

Compared with Lambeth 1968 there was a far greater number of indigenous bishops and far fewer white bishops representing dioceses which were formerly regarded as Mission Areas. Lambeth 1958 probably saw the last of the natural dominance of the Conference by bishops from the West. This was changing ten years ago, and now the spread is truly more indicative of a world-wide Church.

On the domestic front, the work of the City and Town Parishes Commission was terminated on the first day of the general synod. Dr Gordon Perdue retired having served twenty-four years as a bishop, the last twenty-one in Cork. He was succeeded by the Archdeacon of Dublin, the Ven. Samuel Poyntz.

Overshadowing all other events in 1979 was the visit of Pope John Paul II. The sense of anticipation grew as Saturday, 29 September approached. A leading article in *The Irish Times* on the day before described the event as 'a festival of festivals. A massive national outing such as none of us may ever see again and such as none has ever seen before'. And yet, in a real sense it was difficult to be identified totally with the visit. The leader writer concluded his piece by saying, 'And we can sort out the tribalisms later'. I believe that the use of the emotive term 'tribal' did less than justice to sincerely held differences. The visit was linked to the centenary of Knock shrine, and that in itself highlighted the doctrinal and devotional divergence that some, at least, of the minority experienced. I felt compelled to air this in public by a letter to *The Irish Times*.

It was one of the few occasions on which I have taken such a step, and the contrasting responses were interesting. On the Protestant side, I was accused by one man of being an extreme bigot, while a well-known Roman Catholic cleric gently led me to see the role of Marian devotion in the lives of some mutual friends. He also pointed out that the Holy Father had helped to purify and deepen devotion to Mary by directing it more explicitly towards discipleship of Jesus, and referred to the sermon at Knock based on the Cana gospel – 'Whatsoever he shall say to you, do'. In *The Irish Times* during the following week, this emphasis on the centrality of Christ was reckoned by Professor John Barkley, from a Presbyterian perspective, to be the first and most vital feature of the whole visit.

Despite this, I still was compelled to reply that, as I watched and listened to the events at Knock, I felt in a very deep manner (as I had scarcely ever felt before) that I was a stranger in a strange land – 'in' but not 'of' the community. It was a strange feeling of isolation, compounded by the phrase 'Mary, Queen of Ireland'.

There was an eerie feeling in Dublin that morning as tens of thousands made their way to the Phoenix Park from a very early hour. Proceedings began at 7 o'clock and the Holy Father arrived by helicopter at 11.30. He had a punishing schedule, involving visits to Drogheda, Knock, Galway and Limerick, in addition to meeting with representatives of other traditions including bishops and laity of the Church of Ireland. The media coverage of the visit was vast, both before the event and in subsequent analysis. Among a series of 'News Focus' features in *The Irish Times*, Canon Edgar Turner drew out the ecumenical implications of some of the five sermons and six addresses given by the Pope – 30,000 words in all. By way of contrast, he spoke of the Pope of Drogheda, the Pope with the human face, and the Pope of Limerick, the Pope with the marble face of tradition. He concluded the article by saying –

> Though the damp mists and cold rain of Limerick seemed to indicate that a depression was settling in again, yet the bright sunshine and fresh breezes of Drogheda will not be forgotten, and it is from there that a brighter outlook can be seen for the future climate of Irish Christianity.

This hope for the future was referred to by the Bishop of Connor, the Rt Rev. Arthur Butler, in his diocesan synod address just a few days after the Papal visit, when he said –

> We must be glad that he has come and has had such a great welcome and has encouraged and helped the members of his Church by his deeds and words ... There must be very few people indeed who seriously thought that the Pope in a three-day visit would solve our terrible problems. Of course he didn't, but

his impact upon all was such that it is not unreasonable to hope and think that there may now be a strengthening and deepening of the bonds between all who are trying to follow Christ.

It was inevitable that what was scheduled as a pastoral visit should have become a national event. But while all could rejoice, it did highlight the vast denominational imbalance in the south of Ireland. For most of the time this is irrelevant, but there are occasions when it is obvious, and the Papal visit was one such occasion. It is a problem not just for the minority, but also for the majority as horizons are widened, not least by membership of the European Community. Majorities and minorities relate to specific geographical areas, and the more we think of ourselves as Europeans, the less will the national religious division be applicable.

After the initial euphoria, what have been the long-term results of the Papal visit? The observations of an outsider can only be peripheral, but in relation to the words spoken at the time, some comments can be made.

The heartfelt plea to the terrorists at Drogheda has not been matched by a response. Did we all expect too much, or was the negative reaction simply an indication that those involved in violence have become deaf to pleadings from all quarters?

How have the young people of Ireland responded to the words of deep emotion, spoken at Galway – 'Young people of Ireland, I love you'? Certainly not because of his visit, but since it, there has been an alienation of youth from the institutional Church, if conversations with leading Roman Catholic clerics are anything to go by.

At Limerick, there was a reiteration of traditional Roman Catholic ethical teaching, in the context of a discourse on the family on such matters as contraception, abortion and divorce. Since then few would deny the widespread use of contraception and the recognition by many that it is what Archbishop Caird once described as 'an inalienable right'. The question of abortion has been placed before the country on two occasions, and if events have proved anything, it is the complexity of the issue once it is taken out of the realm of theological idealism.

On the matter of divorce, the Government is committed to holding a referendum, which in itself is a step hardly contemplated in 1979.

At Maynooth, the Pope urged those entering the ministry to dress so that they would visibly demonstrate their priesthood. Although regarded by some as almost a trite address, this particular point was, I believe, well made. The clerical uniform identifies the wearer and gives a message. In a sense, it is a method of evangelism, and can provide opportunities for contact in the most unlikely places. It may deter some, but on balance I believe it does more good than the contrary.

The foregoing comments are, of necessity, superficial as coming from outside that tradition which gives allegiance to the Pope. Perhaps from within, one could speak of a deepening of spirituality, and the whole tone of the sermon in Phoenix Park was geared to that end. Or was it that the occasion overshadowed the message?

One small postscript to the Papal visit. It was a staunch member of the Church of Ireland who was called on to help organise the stewarding operation in the Phoenix Park. And so, in some small measure (apart from our prayers), we had a hand in ensuring the success of a unique event in Irish history.

While the visit of the Holy Father may have claimed the media attention, 1979 was not without other more domestic events. The Anglican Consultative Council held its fourth meeting in London, Ontario; Mr Harry Roberts became chief officer of the RCB, and the question of the ordination of women was referred to diocesan synods. However, dominating home affairs was the report of the Priorities Committee, *First of All*, which was described by the Primate as 'rich in ideas and practical in its recommendations'.

The nine-man committee (there were no ladies on it), headed by the then Bishop of Derry, Dr Eames, had been set up by the RCB in April 1977 to consider the priorities involved in looking after the material resources of the Church, including the role and responsibility of the Representative Body. General synod in the same year passed two resolutions expanding the committee's brief and, in February 1978, the RCB agreed, on the basis of an interim report, that the committee should continue its work along the very broad lines that had evolved as they progressed.

The Priorities Commission report was widely circulated and discussed throughout the Church. The opening two lines of the preface became the text for many a speech at Church gatherings, 'The first priority of the Church of Ireland is spiritual – not material' and 'The history of our Church is an inspiration – not a burden'. Every area of Church life was examined, and recommendations made. The report still repays careful reading after fourteen years.

Like many others, our own parish of Zion studied the report at various levels, including diocesan synodsmen, select vestry, organisation leaders and at a general meeting of parishioners. Subsequently, comments were submitted and these included – the Church of Ireland has a product (the gospel) which needs to be sold, and not taken for granted; the need to have a vision of where the Church is going; the question of the ministry needs to be thought out carefully in relation to such matters as sabbatical leave and time for reflection; the need for a retreat house, not just for groups, but where individuals could go for short periods of quiet. Those with comparatively long memories will recall the resource that Murlough House was, and the debt owed to Bishop Mitchell when he was in Down and Dromore. I well recall very profitable parish retreats in that picturesque setting near Dundrum in Co. Down when I was curate in Rathfarnham.

Much of what was recommended in the report needed finance, and so, that committee recommended the establishment of a new fund to be called the Priorities Fund, through which the Church could show, by its support, that the true priorities had been established. This fund was inaugurated at the pre-general synod service in St Patrick's Cathedral the following year. The cynics delighted in pointing out that, having identified the first priority of the Church of Ireland as spiritual, what do we do but set up a fund! However, the fund has enabled the Church to address the spiritual needs of its people in a comprehensive way through support in such areas as ministry, education and social responsibility. Careful scrutiny is made to ensure that money received from the dioceses each year is disbursed in the original spirit of the fund, and before allocations are made the approval of the standing committee of the general synod must be obtained.

It would have been unusual if the Priorities Commission report had received universal approval, and the group most critical at the time was the Church of Ireland Youth Council. In their official response they said, 'We are deeply disappointed at the fact that ministry among young people receives hardly a passing mention in the report'. And they went on to call for greater involvement of laity and, in particular, women in the life of the Church. It was pointed out at the time that the report was looking at the overall life of the Church and charting a direction, rather than focusing on specific groups. It was intended that all those engaged in the work of the Church of Ireland would gain from the insights in the report, and this in fact has been the case if one views the life of the Church over the last fourteen years against the contents of *First of All*. Today the CIYC receives substantial financial support from the Priorities Fund, and that in itself is a recognition by the Church of the importance of youth work.

The report also contained a mass of statistical material which, while now outdated, is none the less interesting. It revealed, for example, a decline in membership from 403,500 recorded in *Administration 1967* to 375,600 in *First of All*, a drop of 7 per cent, although it was pointed out that this could partly be explained by a non-standard approach to statistics, some parishes/dioceses not including people whose Church connection is nominal. Church statistics are notorious for their lack of uniformity. Often they depend on the purpose for which they are being supplied. There used to be a Dublin parish where the parochial statistics were inflated each year on the rural dean's returns by the inclusion of the patients in a hospital within the parish!

The retirement of Archbishop Simms took place in February 1980. For eleven years he had led the Church of Ireland through a period of great political turbulence. His successor in Armagh was Bishop John Armstrong. Referring to Dr Simms in his general synod address he said, 'There were times when only George Simms could have survived without tempers being frayed'. Can anyone recall a time when George Simms' temper was frayed? He had that great capacity to absorb comment and, often by his delayed response, to disarm those opposed to him. His retirement was an active one and he was much sought after as a preacher and speaker, while his lecture on the *Book of Kells* commanded enthusiastic audiences wherever he delivered it. He also continued to be involved directly with the theological journal, *Search*, as chairman of the editorial committee and as President of the Sunday School Society of Ireland. It was during his term of office, for example, that the three-year faith education programme, *Growing Together*, was produced by the society. He was also theological consultant for the book *Sing and Pray*, a companion volume to *Growing Together* and *Primary R.E.*, the syllabus produced by the board of education of the general synod.

John Armstrong was a different type of primate. His first presidential address was more directive than usual. He had his mind firmly fixed on the production of the *Alternative Prayer Book*, and speaking of the Bishops' Appeal he said – 'We must give that others may live'. This reflected his interest in the needs of the Third World which had been heightened by his many overseas trips to represent the Church of Ireland. The Bishops' Appeal committee had been set up in 1971 to respond to relief and development needs, and Bishop Armstrong had been its first chairman. In many ways, it is the Church of Ireland's barometer in its claim to be a caring Church, and from an initial response of £21,000 in 1972, it has risen to well over £600,000 in 1992. While this increase to some extent reflects the tragic situation in parts of Africa, where famine and civil strife have caused such havoc in recent years, it is also an indication of genuine practical concern arising out of Christian commitment. While this increase is welcomed, there is a fear that it may affect contributions to the traditional missionary societies which for generations have served the Church of Ireland with distinction. There will always be the need for primary evangelism if the Church is to be true to Our Lord's command to make disciples of all nations. The difficulty is to get the balance right at any given time, and there is no doubt that at present the heartstrings of humanity are being touched by the much publicised plight of those in such countries as Somalia and the Sudan, not to mention Rumania and the former Yugoslavia. Later in 1990, on being elected to the board of Christian Aid, I was to become even more aware of the needs of the poor of the world and the complexities and misunderstandings than can arise when the Church seeks to live out the Gospel.

In 1980 the Select Committee on the Ordination of Women to the Priesthood was able to report a very positive response from the dioceses. Overall, the majority in favour was 74.8 per cent (63.9 clerical and 83.8 laity). In Cork, Cloyne and Ross the percentages in favour were – clerical 66.1 per cent and laity 76.8 per cent. However, when a resolution was put to the general synod to obtain leave for the introduction of a bill in 1981 making provision for the ordination of women to the priesthood, it was rejected, having failed to obtain a two-thirds majority of the clergy. The actual voting was 61.7 per cent clerical and 76.84 per cent laity. Instead, a resolution was put in 1981 to introduce a bill in 1982 allowing for the ordination of women to the diaconate. This was passed by the necessary two-thirds majority in each case, but when the bill came to the House it was withdrawn for technical reasons amid scenes of great emotion. There was no doubting the correctness of this step, but at the time it appeared to some as a ploy to forestall legislation.

In 1983 a new resolution was put and passed and in 1984 the bill opening the way for the ordination of women to the diaconate was passed. Five more years were to go by before a resolution was introduced to the general synod of 1989 that leave be granted for the introduction of a bill to the general synod of 1990 to enable women to be ordained as priests and bishops. This resolution was passed by the necessary two-thirds majorities – 73.6 per cent clerical and 86.8 per cent laity. And so the scene was set for a decisive vote in synod in 1990. In a sense, the debate lacked originality. The arguments had been repeated many times before. But there was no doubting the sincerity of all who spoke. Those who were present are unlikely to forget the atmosphere as the Primate (Archbishop Eames) called the members to prayer and requested that there be no applause when the result was announced. The *Journal of the General Synod* records the historic outcome in typical factual terms – 'As a result of a division the third reading was declared passed by the required majorities. Voting: Clerical – Ayes 126, Nos 55. Lay – Ayes 172, Nos 29'. Translated into percentages that means 69.6 per cent of the clergy in favour and 85.6 per cent of the laity. The *Journal* then records that the House adjourned at 1.05p.m. in order to allow the House of Bishops to vote.

It was the first time since disestablishment that the House of Bishops had exercised this right. When the synod resumed at 1.13p.m. the president declared that a majority of the House of Bishops was in favour of the motion. That there was no public episcopal vote was regarded by some as a shortcoming in the whole process, but the standing orders of synod are quite specific. In any case, where there is a majority quoted it provides an interesting sphere of speculation, and for the remainder of the synod there was plenty of that, to be sure.

Archbishop Armstrong would have regarded himself as on the evangelical wing of the Church and his endorsement of the Renewal Conference in Dublin in November 1980 was enthusiastic. The leaders of the conference were two well-known and much travelled speakers – Dr Michael Marshall and the Rev. Michael Harper. This was followed by a similar conference in Belfast two years later which was addressed by the then Archbishop of Cape Town, the Most Rev. Bill Burnett, one of the best known international leaders of the charismatic movement. Indeed, a feature of Church life at the time was this movement. It cut right across denominational lines but appeared to find wider acceptance in the Roman Catholic Church than in the Church of Ireland. Perhaps this has to do with perception or numbers, but within our own Church one thinks of the movement in terms of enthusiastic individuals rather than overall integration.

The appointment of Dr Armstrong to Armagh was to have a knock-on effect, but little did I realise that it would affect me personally. The vacancy in Cashel and Ossory was filled by the Archdeacon of Dublin, the Ven. Noel Willoughby. On Maundy Thursday 1980 I was called to the See House and

invited by Archbishop McAdoo to take over the post of Archdeacon. It proved to be the beginning of one of the most demanding but satisfying periods of my ministry.

When I announced the appointment to the parish I said
that there were three prime requirements – a sympathetic parish, a patient wife and a reliable colleague. I was fortunate in
having all three. I was also conscious that I was entering into a
line of illustrious predecessors whose mould had been broken
by the appointment of the comparatively youthful vicar of St
Anne's, Dr Samuel Poyntz, by Archbishop Buchanan in 1974.

If an archdeacon has certain requirements at the parish
level, there is one top priority at the diocesan level, and that is
a supportive group of clergy. That too I was fortunate in having. As the eyes and ears of the bishop, an archdeacon is constantly in touch with clergy. He is a conduit for concerns and
an interpreter of policy.

Within the Church of Ireland, and unlike many other
Anglican provinces, archdeacons are also parish clergy. Only
once, from 1969–79 in the Diocese of Connor, has there been a
full-time archdeacon, and the non-repetition of the experiment
seems to indicate that it was not regarded with total satisfaction. One could easily float between the episcopal and the
parochial without any real base, although full attention could
be given to the task in hand.

The danger for the part-time archdeacon, especially in one
of the larger dioceses, is that he too floats between the episcopal and the parochial, forever seeking to prioritise his parochial duties, while at the same time doing justice to the diocesan dimension.

In the Dublin of the 1980s this was highlighted by the
great emphasis on parochial reorganisation. The archdeacon
chaired the relevant committee (it was once reckoned that an
archdeacon of Dublin was on over fifty committees!) which
met with representatives from a great number of parishes. It
was vitally relevant but time-consuming work as we tried to
chart a course for the Church in the rapidly expanding suburbs, matched by the fast declining inner city population.

In terms of job satisfaction, one of the happiest events
each year was the clergy conference. In Dublin it had been

inaugurated by Archbishop Buchanan and Archdeacon
Poyntz in the mid-1970s at Carrig Eden in Greystones. Early
on, it became known as 'the bicycle rally'. Dr Buchanan had
extolled the virtues of using the bicycle as a means of transport, hence the nickname. Initially, the conference was viewed
with some suspicion. Clergy are an independent lot, and while
gregarious up to a point, once it goes beyond being voluntary,
resistance can be encountered. However, it soon became a
feature of diocesan life (as is the case in every diocese now).
Early on, it moved from the restrictive shores of Greystones to
the more liberal pastures of Dundrum, and for some years has
been located at Gort Mhuire Conference Centre. It was here
also that the standing committee of the general synod held a
residential conference in 1983 to examine the future role of the
Church of Ireland in this island.

It is sometimes said that there are two types of bishop –
those that have been archdeacons and those that haven't. Certainly to be Archdeacon of Dublin provides valuable opportunities of insight into the life of the Church, not least the immense burden carried by the archbishop. When this is combined with a task, such as joint-chairmanship of the Anglican-
Roman Catholic International Commission, it calls for organisation and self-discipline of the highest order. The publication of the final report of ARCIC 1 in 1982 brought to an end a
twelve-year period of sustained pressure for Dr McAdoo, although the aftermath of the report meant his ongoing involvement for a considerable period, as comments and reactions were sought from many quarters.

One of the fears in the early 1980s was that the distinctive
voice of the Church of Ireland, in relation to Northern Ireland,
was not being heard on the world scene, especially in America. With this in mind, a delegation headed by Dr Eames visited the United States in 1981. The concern being expressed
highlighted the dilemma that can arise – how far can a Church
of Ireland view be totally equated with a pan-Protestant view?
The fact that the delegation represented the whole of Ireland
was important. It was a reminder that while the media may
concentrate on the role of the Churches in the north, there is
an influential Church of Ireland presence in the south also.

The Church of Ireland is strong on reports, and yet another was presented to the general synod in 1981, *Ministry Today – a Calling for All*. It was the fruit of a commission, with Bishop Edwin Owen (Limerick and Killaloe) as chairman, which had been set up in 1979 by the RCB, to examine the implications of Chapters 4 and 5 of the Priorities Committee report, that is, those dealing with ministry and flexibility.

It turned out to be a far-reaching and comprehensive report dealing with every possible aspect of ministry, starting from a theological understanding of the subject. Here it was pointed out that such an understanding implies that the study begins not simply with a critique of current difficulties and problems, but rather with God and with His purpose for His people. Speaking at a meeting of parishioners in Zion, Bishop Owen referred to the report as 'a recipe for revolution', and suggested to those present that 'We're living in the rubble of a disintegrating society'. Whatever about society at large, and there are alarming indications that the bishop may have been right, there is no doubt that the whole question of ministry needs to be re-examined as we approach the twenty-first century. The expectations of many are still set in the Church of fifty years ago. And so it is not just a case of another commission making recommendations, or even the general synod passing legislation; there must be a process of education carried out at grass roots level so that people realise that, in terms of ministry, life can never be the same again. It will not be an easy task, but unless we move out of the moulds of the past, the decreasing number of stipendiary clergy will become more and more frustrated, and parishioners will grow disillusioned.

At the same general synod, a commission on communication was set up –

> ... to examine Church of Ireland communications policy both within the Church of Ireland, and, from it, outwards, with a view to making recommendations aimed at using to the optimum our structure, our ready-made communications network, and the talents of our people both lay and clerical.

The report set a headline, as might be expected, in that it was eminently readable. In other words, it communicated to its readers. While it is dangerous to take isolated quotations out of context, two brief paragraphs are worth repeating. The first is on page 21 –

> The people in the broadcasting media are professionals. They have a right to expect professionalism from the Church in performing the task which it declares to be of prime importance – the proclamation of the Gospel.

Here we come up against the whole question of selection. Who should broadcast? One can only become professional in the sense indicated in the report by frequent exposure. Training will of course help, but some of the best known broadcasters have been those for whom training would have been a disaster. They were naturals. For example, I am not sure that George Simms ever attended a training course. Have we many natural broadcasters in the Church of Ireland today? If we have, then surely we should be promoting them, not least in the expanding sphere of local radio. Whether we like it or not, it is the age of the personality, not a popular concept in the Church of Ireland. Yet, if we are to respond to the challenges and opportunities of the broadcasting media, we will need to jettison the representative approach so beloved at administrative level, and concentrate on those who have this particular gift. If there had been broadcasting in the time of St Paul, he might well have included it in the gifts of the Spirit!

The second quotation is on page 35:

> We would argue that we cannot continue to tack communication on to the workload of the Church by the cheapest possible means.

In practice, this often means tacking it on to the workload of the clergy, and given the diminishing number of clergy, the folly of this is not hard to imagine.

On the episcopal front, 1981 saw the retirement of two members of the bench – Bishop Moore and Bishop Butler, while during the same year the Church of Ireland was honoured by a visit from the Archbishop of Canterbury, Dr Robert

Runcie. He was accompanied by the Advisor, Terry Waite. Little did anyone anticipate the drama that would unfold within a few short years, and the central role he would play. The following year, the Falklands/Malvinas War was in the news and, at a service at the end of hostilities, the archbishop incurred the displeasure of Mrs Thatcher by the less than triumphalist tone of his sermon.

Two events of contrasting style occurred during 1981 in Northern Ireland, the completion of St Anne's Cathedral and the notorious H-Block protest. There is no doubt which received the most publicity at the time, but the question is – which will be of more lasting significance?

Speaking at the general synod of 1982, Archbishop Armstrong dwelt on two continuing problems – alcohol addiction and unemployment. In the same presidential speech, he gave indications of removal from the Synod Hall. Little did the delegates fully realise that this would be the last year in the traditional surroundings. 1983 was to see the move to the RDS. At that first meeting, a motion was passed permitting the synod to meet in Belfast or 'elsewhere in Ireland'. As a result of this, there have been two meetings in Belfast and one is scheduled for Cork in 1994.

1983 was highlighted by the contentious campaign surrounding the referendum on the eighth amendment to the Constitution. It came to be characterised as the Pro-Life Amendment, and commenting on this, the Role of the Church report observed, 'The Pro-Life campaign used a title which by implication excluded many citizens in the Republic who abhorred abortion'. As events were tragically to prove, the warning by the Church of Ireland that the wording could prove ambiguous was justified, but few people listen to the minority voice when emotion is fuelled by religious fervour.

Later that year, the House of Bishops responded to the then recently published *Roman Catholic Directory on Marriage*. They stressed the need for equality of conscience in all aspects of an inter-Church marriage. Referring to this in their report the following year, the Role of the Church Committee said, 'This is the nub of the issue – a basic human right which must be acknowledged for the sake of the partners in an inter-

Church marriage.'

During August 1983, the death occurred in Oxford of
Archbishop McCann. His passing went unnoticed by many.
Yet in his day he was a man of immense stature in the Church
of Ireland. His preaching had an oratorical ring about it that
few could match, and his general synod addresses had a practical content that reflected his journey through the ranks.
When he spoke, it was out of experience at the grass-roots
level. He was not a media man and was happy to leave that
side of things to the Archbishop of Dublin. He appeared to be
a shy man, and perhaps he was lucky to exercise his oversight
at a time when the media men and women were less demanding than they are today.

The move to the RDS not only meant the loss of the traditional debating chamber, but also the loss of the time-
honoured Eucharist in Christ Church Cathedral on the first
morning of the synod. It was never going to be easy to com-
pensate for that. The service is the responsibility of the Archbishop of Dublin and it was decided to hold it in the RDS. Reactions were mixed and, as is usual in such cases, those opposed made most noise. It was inevitable that there would be
teething problems given the nature of the building. But it did
at least link work and worship in a very real way, and five
years later, at the Lambeth Conference, the setting for worship
was not dissimilar as we met in the main conference hall at the
University of Kent. It could well be that we need to take a long
hard look at the overall pattern of general synod worship. The
cost factor means that more and more people are travelling on
Tuesday morning with a consequent reduction in the numbers
at both the pre-synod service and the opening Eucharist. It is
difficult to alter familiar patterns but the timing, content and
structure of our two main services would benefit from close
scrutiny.

A number of important events marked 1984, but the year
began on a sad note when, in February, Archbishop Buchanan
died after a long and trying illness. His passing removed one
of the outstanding pastoral figures of the Church.

Much attention was focused on the New Ireland Forum
whose report was published on 2 May 1984. The Church of

Ireland delegation to the forum had been led by Bishop Poyntz, chairman of the Role of the Church Committee. In all, 317 submissions were received by the forum, which was a measure of the hope that was enshrined in its proceedings. Although some doubted the wisdom of Church of Ireland involvement, on balance it was felt that more could be achieved by being part of the game than standing on the sideline. Speaking of the event at synod, David Bleakely, with typical ear-catching phraseology, reminded members that 'We in Ireland are caught in one of history's hurricanes'.

St Luke's Day (18 October) marked the launching of *The Alternative Prayer Book 1984,* and in many ways was the climax of Archbishop Armstrong's archiepiscopate. Representatives from every diocese gathered in Armagh for the inauguration service in St Patrick's Cathedral. The sermon was to have been delivered by the Primate of Wales but due to bad weather he was unable to make the journey. The Irish Primate read the sermon instead. In it was spelled out one of the dangers inherent in having alternative prayer books, that of division at the local level. It was pointed out that in Wales there is but one book. To some extent, his point has been proved. It used to be stressed that one of the attractions of Anglicanism was the binding cord of liturgy contained in the *Book of Common Prayer*. Now the emphasis is on choice and flexibility. However, this must be kept within allowable bounds. Those in the pew have a right to expect conformity and not the idiosyncrasies of individual clergy or attempts to marry the ancient and the modern forms of service. Very few of us have the liturgical expertise to make a good job of it. As a means of introducing the *APB* to a wider audience, the choir and congregation of Zion parish took part in a televised service from RTE shortly after the launching of the book in Armagh.

The Sunday School Society of Ireland has always played an important role in the life of the Church of Ireland even providing Sunday school by post for those in isolated areas. 1984 marked the 175th anniversary of the society and it was celebrated by a pageant at the National Concert Hall. The society was under the chairmanship of Mr Michael Coote, and when he retired his place was taken by a Zion parishioner, Mr

Eric Hunt.

1985 marked the retirement of Dr McAdoo as Archbishop of Dublin. His twenty-four years as a bishop had been marked by an unflinching devotion to the ethos of the Church of Ireland and, as a scholar of international reputation, his theological contribution to the world church has been immense as an interpreter of Anglicanism. Happily, since his retirement this work has continued unabated. As he might say himself, he is still scribbling. Those who worked closest to him at diocesan level were equally conscious of his pastoral concern and administrative ability, especially in the conduct of staff meetings and interviews. He was succeeded by the Bishop of Meath and Kildare, the Most Rev. Donald Caird who, like Dr McAdoo, is an Irish scholar and fluent speaker.

The synod that year was to be the last presided over by Archbishop Armstrong before he retired, and it was therefore appropriate that it should be held in Belfast, Dr Armstrong's home town. It was characterised by the number of women members – sixty, the highest number ever. At the synod, one felt a genuine sense of gladness that the decision had been taken to move north. Unfortunately, a familiar dark cloud hung over proceedings. On the Monday, many travelling north by road had to be directed by Carlingford because of a bomb outside Newry which had killed four people. It was a sad reminder for some from the peaceful pastures of the south of the stark reality of life on parts of the same island. It was the fond hope, not yet realised, that the Anglo-Irish Agreement, signed later that year on 15 November, would help to relieve the situation.

On 7 February 1986 the House of Bishops elected the Bishop of Down and Dromore, the Rt Rev. R.H.A. Eames as Archbishop of Armagh, Primate of All Ireland and Metropolitan. In his first synod address the following May, he outlined three main areas of concern: Northern Ireland with its two traditions, the family and marriage, and inter-Church relations including a consideration of the final report of ARCIC 1. He took the opportunity to state clearly that the Church of Ireland does not advocate divorce, but went on to say:

We see divorce accompanied by the strongest safeguards within society as an option for those who after a considerable period of time find that all means of reconciliation have failed and that their marriage has irretrievably ended.

In view of the Government's commitment to hold a referendum on divorce, this statement assumes added significance.

It was at the 1986 general synod that a bill was passed to provide for a reduction in the number of churches open for public worship, and the setting up of the Commission on Church Buildings. It was proposed by the Bishop of Cork, Dr Poyntz, and seconded by Mr F.G.G. Quayle, and resulted from the deliberations of an advisory committee set up in 1984 following a request from the diocesan council of Cork, Cloyne and Ross. The following year, the commission was invited into Meath and Kildare, and in 1988 Cork followed suit.

A feature of presidential addresses at synod has been their gradual lengthening, certainly since 1953, and in 1987 Dr Eames delivered what was without doubt the longest during that period. The general theme was 'Looking Forward', and he asked the question 'Who are we?' In reply he said:

> The key to that much discussed phrase 'the ethos of the Church of Ireland' must lie in our tradition of moderation, charity and loyalty to what we perceive as our response as Anglicans to the call of God in Ireland.

Turning to spirituality, he referred to the 'traditional weakness of the Church of Ireland – nominal membership'. It was an address which should be required reading in any future debate on the role of the Church of Ireland and its contribution to Irish society.

At the same synod, AIDS was first mentioned in the Role of the Church report, an indication that Ireland was beginning to feel the effects of that terrible global scourge. Voices from within the Church advocate monogamous relationships in the context of the marriage bond, but it is not a popular remedy. Neither is it the complete remedy, but it is one which many have in their own hands, and the other side of the tragic coin must surely be the unwillingness of so many to exercise self-control. The fact that the centenary of the Mothers' Union in Ireland was celebrated the same year highlighted the value of stable family life.

The life of the Church would be immeasurably duller if there were no hymns. They are an integral part of our worship, and for some they are the main transmitters of theological ideas. Therefore, a significant resolution passed at the 1987 synod was that setting up the Hymn Book Revision Committee. With unaccustomed alacrity for a Church committee, they decided what should be done, and 1990 saw the production of *Irish Church Praise*, a supplement to the 1960 edition of the *Irish Church Hymnal*. It has been very well received throughout the Church of Ireland and beyond.

At a personal level, two contrasting events marked 1987. The first occurred when I became ill starting out on holiday and found myself in hospital in Newport, South Wales. Due to the good offices of Canon Norman Autton, who is well known in Ireland as a lecturer on pastoral care and related subjects, my wife and I were put in contact with the vicar of St Mark's, Newport, the Rev. Kenneth Sharpe. He and his wife, Christine, immediately took Eileen into their rectory and treated her as one of the family. On my release after a week, we stayed with Kenneth and Christine for another week, again as part of the household. It was a wonderful experience of Christian hospitality, and something we shall never forget. Through it we have become close friends, and out of the most unlikely situation emerged a time of great blessing.

The second event occurred almost five months later, on 23 November to be precise, when the Episcopal Electoral College saw fit to elect me Bishop of Cork, Cloyne and Ross in succession to Bishop Poyntz who had been appointed by the House of Bishops to the Diocese of Connor. So personally unexpected was the election that my parting words to my wife on leaving for the Electoral College, of which I was a member, were to assure her that I would be back home at about 4.30 in the afternoon. Instead, I was phoning her around that time to break the news of impending upheaval.

~ 9 ~

The Deep South

HAVING SERVED IN the United Diocese of Dublin and Glendalough for thirty-two years and in the same parish for the last sixteen years, the move to Cork was viewed with no little apprehension. Apart altogether from the nature of the work, there was the totally different milieu to be taken into consideration. I was encouraged by the deluge of good wishes from a variety of people. On the ecumenical level, I was heartened by the first letter I received which was from the Roman Catholic Bishop of Cloyne, the Most Rev. John Magee. For a number of years he had acted as Papal Secretary and, in extending good wishes to Eileen and me, he expressed the hope that we could share our pastoral experience.

However, it was from two Church of Ireland episcopal letters that I derived most encouragement. They came from one serving and one retired bishop, but both had the same basic message – always be mindful of the grace of orders. In others words, whatever the weight of office, God's grace will be sufficient. During the past five years I have often recalled that message of assurance and thanked God for the insight of those two men.

A letter from a former colleague contained a comment over which I have often pondered since. With characteristic perception he wrote: 'I hope you will be allowed to choose your own agenda'. As a certain chat show host might say, 'Think about it'. So often a bishop's agenda is not his own. It is bound up with, even dictated by, the structures which he is expected to serve, and the expectations of the Church at large.

My first task within minutes of being elected was to meet the press – all two of them! Two questions stick in my mind. 'Will you have as high a profile as your predecessor?' and 'What are your hopes for the diocese?' To the first I suggested that profile depended to some extent on the media itself, while to the second I responded that my hope would be to have a happy diocese. My feeling is that both replies were unexpected and viewed as disappointing. Yet, what greater hope can one have in life, either as an individual or as a member of a diocesan family, than to experience a deep-seated happiness based on a right relationship with God through Jesus Christ. That may not be the stuff of media headlines, but I believe it should be the goal of all our striving.

As with most other positions in the Church of Ireland, very little is done to prepare a bishop for his future work. Once elected and the date of consecration set, you are very much on your own. In my own case, Christmas, with its hectic parochial schedule, intervened and preparations were sandwiched into a few short weeks in January. The mantle of episcopacy is somehow expected to descend on those newly elected. To add to the sense of haste, my father-in-law died on a bleak December day when we were in Cork viewing our future home.

Although I had come up through the system, and had acted as commissary for some months in Dublin, the most difficult task was to prepare mentally for the work of a bishop. I was fascinated to read that the first lady diocesan bishop from New Zealand spent a month in Scotland by way of preparation before her consecration. I spent two days on retreat in Gort Mhuire endeavouring to unwind in peaceful surroundings which I had come to appreciate at our diocesan clergy conferences. It was only eighteen months later that I had the opportunity to attend a bishops' training course in England, organised by the Archbishop of Canterbury's Advisor for Bishops' Ministry, the Rev. Dr Norman Todd. In a sense, it was a help to have been in office for a year-and-a-half, but nonetheless I believe there is a real gap in our training programme when it comes to the episcopate, even though it has been on the agenda of the last three Lambeth conferences.

Certain elements in the course organised by Dr Todd are worth recording. It consisted of two week-long sessions separated by a month. By way of preparation, we had to keep a six-week diary of all activities, broken into half-hour periods. This underlined for me the amount of travelling involved. Having come from a parish where all the plant was conveniently situated in the one place, I found the extended travel disconcerting at first. It's no mean journey from Castletownbere to Cork when you have been used to walking home in 60 seconds flat.

On the course, three sections were devoted to management style input. It was not a matter of saying, this is what you should do, but rather: this is how it is done in business, is there anything the Church can learn from us? While recognising the limitations in a Church setting, there is no doubt that this type of approach can be of great benefit, and a certain number of clergy are availing of courses which are on offer.

For the last three days of the second week, wives were present. This was a recognition of the vital role wives play. As in rectory households, so in bishops' houses, wives are often the first contact. Occasionally, they may find themselves in the firing line, although this is more likely to happen in Ireland than in the populous dioceses of England.

In recent years, in the Theological College, more thought has been put into preparing clergy wives for what lies ahead. There are obviously different levels of perception, and some couples speak of a joint ministry. While much can be done together and by way of mutual support, there has to be a clear understanding that only one partner is ordained, and there is a distinctive level of ministry which he/she alone can perform. This is something which parishioners have a right to expect, especially in terms of confidentiality.

One of the most interesting lectures given during the two weeks was by the Bishop of Salisbury, the Rt Rev. John Austin Baker, on the Theology of the Episcopate. It is a paper to which I have returned many times for reflection. In the course of it, Bishop Baker posed a question, 'Does God want bishops?' After a lengthy dissertation, he arrived at an affirmative answer. However, his 'yes' was qualified by the caveat that they must be bishops who seek to reflect the mind of Christ.

In pondering over Bishop Baker's question, I have found it helpful to do so under certain headings, while at the same time attempting to relate them to our own diocese in particular.

1. The first heading is that of *WORSHIP*.

From the earliest times, the bishop as local head of the Church has presided at its liturgy, especially the Eucharist, and it is one of my great joys as a bishop to preside at Holy Communion when I visit a parish. As the Church grew and expanded, this function was delegated to the local presbyter or priest. Unfortunately, today our worship is suffering because some clergy are caught up in the helter skelter of the Sunday schedule. If worship is at the core of the Church's reason for existence, then we must be careful not to demean it by undue haste.

2. The second heading is *REPRESENTATION*.

The bishop is a representative figure in a number of senses.

(a)   He represents the Church of Ireland to the community at large. This can be time-consuming, but important. On occasions, it provides an opportunity to outline the Church of Ireland's position on some subject. It is an indication that the Church of Ireland wants to be, and indeed is, a part of the broader community. It is also a token of support for those who often play a leading role in community affairs.

(b)   In the second place, the bishop represents the diocese to the wider Church, both in denominational and ecumenical terms. While in many ways the parish is the focus of the Church's life, the diocese is the prime administrative unit, and the bishop must be concerned for the overall good of the diocese.

(c)   However, the bishop also represents the wider Church to the diocese. He is a bishop of the Church of God and, as such, must seek to enlarge the vision of those specifically committed to his charge. Because of our small numbers there is a danger that we will become caught up in a philosophy of decline. But set in a wider context we are part of the world-wide Church of God which is increasing at the rate of 80,000 members a day. It is the task of the bishop to remind people of this wider context. In some cases this is achieved by means of a link diocese, and in the case of Cork this relationship is being developed with the Diocese of Swansea and Brecon.

3. The third heading is *OVERSIGHT*.

This thought is implicit in the word 'episcopal' whose root meaning is 'oversight'. This relates especially to the clergy. The bishop is *pastor pastorum*, pastor of the pastors. That must always be one of his chief tasks, especially at a time when stress has been identified as a real factor in clerical life.

Oversight, however, is not confined to clergy. At each institution the rector receives his cure of souls in partnership with the bishop. To quote from the new institution service: 'I confer on you the care of God's people in this parish which is entrusted both to you and to me within the body of Christ'. How does one exercise this dual oversight?

I believe it can be done by a specific type of visitation, embracing both the work of the clergy and the life of the parish, during which clergy, based on a short questionnaire, have an opportunity to discuss their work, openly and in some depth. It is vital that clergy (and bishops) engage in some type of assessment, not as a form of threat, but as a means of sharpening up their ministry. This is a theme to which the Archbishop of Canterbury, Dr Carey, has returned over and over again. In this, we can learn from the business world, where targets are set and performance is evaluated on a regular basis. It is all too easy for the Church to drift on a wave of complacency. As a public representative said to me at the time of the local elections – 'You know, Bishop, you're lucky, you don't have to face the electorate.' Perhaps as clergy we don't, but that should in no way dull our sense of purpose.

Nevertheless, oversight is not an easy concept to unravel in the context of Anglicanism. It is bound up with synodical government. The bishop is a bishop in synod, and those who exercise episcopal oversight are no less under the constraints of synodical decisions. This is an area where confusion can arise, especially if the overriding perception of a bishop is that of an old-style prelate. Pastoral oversight and synodical legislation do not always make for a happy marriage. I sometimes recall the words of Dag Hammarskjöld. Writing as secretary general of the United Nations, he said: 'Your position never gives you the right to command. It only imposes on you the duty of so living your life that others can receive your orders without being humiliated.'

4. The fourth heading is *TEACHING.*

In the questions put to a bishop at his consecration, teaching or instructing has a high priority: 'In your ministry will you expound the Scriptures and teach that doctrine?'

However, not only is a bishop called to be a teacher himself, he must encourage others to do the same. If we, as members of the Church of Ireland, want to have a role in helping to develop the Ireland of tomorrow, we much be prepared to come to grips with the complex issues of today. We do so in the light of the principles which we as a Church espouse – for example, recognition that the world is God's world and we as his stewards have a responsibility for the environment, an acceptance of standards of integrity in commercial dealing, a practical concern for the poor and the marginalised worldwide, and a sympathetic regard for those caught in the complicated web of modern society, symbolised by such factors as marriage breakdown and AIDS.

It is only as we deepen our knowledge and understanding of these issues, and couple this with a search for the will of God, that we can make a distinctive contribution to the future of society. But it is all bound up with the teaching ministry which must have its rationale in the role of the bishop as teacher.

5. The fifth heading is *UNITY.*

The bishop should be the focus of unity in a diocese. To quote the Bishop of Salisbury again, 'It is the bishop who sets the tone and calls the people of Christ out of the parochialism to which they are naturally and understandably liable'. Parochial attachment is a necessary and healthy feature of the Church of Ireland. But it becomes unhealthy when it degenerates into a type of congregationalism that is blinkered. It is the duty of the bishop to bring the diocesan perspective to bear on Church life within his diocese, just as it is his duty to reflect the diocesan concerns in the central councils of the Church.

There is also the wider context of unity in terms of our relationships with other Churches, especially in the mainline traditions. Here too it is the duty of the bishop to promote that wider unity of believers for which Christ prayed that they all may be one. When enthusiasm in this respect begins to flag, some words from the rule of the Taizé Community are encouraging: 'Never resign yourself to the scandal of the separation of Christians – be consumed with burning zeal for the unity of the Body of Christ.'

6. The sixth heading is *MISSION*.

It is the duty of the bishop to promote the mission or outreach of the Church in the widest possible context. He does this in response to Our Lord's parting words – 'Go therefore and make disciples of all nations', and Ireland, in the old-style missionary sense of sending people overseas, has a first-rate track record. This theme of outreach was underlined at the 1988 Lambeth Conference in the call to make the closing years of this century a Decade of Evangelism. All the Churches of the Anglican Communion have been urged to move the thrust of their ministry from nurture to outreach.

Within the Church of Ireland, this is proving to be a difficult task. For years the emphasis has been on nurturing our own members, and understandably so in a context where the vast majority of people would claim to be Christian. Unlike many countries overseas, Ireland has never been viewed as a field for primary evangelism, and those who proselytise are viewed with distaste. However, many are asking if we are not witnessing a changing situation at the present time where, in addition to falling church attendance, the core values of Christianity, such as honesty, integrity and purity, are no longer the norms in society. It could well be that this is the area that needs to be addressed in the Decade of Evangelism, rather than any narrow individualistic emphasis on personal salvation. In searching for the right approach, there is one word used over and over again. It is 'vision'. I am constantly being told that the Church, the diocese, the parish, must have a vision, and perhaps the most overused text of the Decade to date is: 'Where there is no vision, the people perish.'

What is that vision we are all encouraged to espouse? I receive many suggestions through my letter box from a variety of agencies. But the definition I like best comes from the present Archbishop of Canterbury. Speaking to his diocesan synod of Bath and Wells in 1989 he said this:

> Now vision is a most overdone word; What does it mean? Yes, we know it comes from the root 'to see'. But it means, in Christian thought, the capacity to enter into God's plans for his people; to think with the boldness and courage of the children of God; to dare to reach out and discover God's will.

Worship, representation, oversight, teaching, unity, mission – these are six broad categories within which a bishop exercises his ministry. But a bishop never walks alone. He must have a team, indeed more than one team. At the diocesan level, there are the clergy who work in the parishes and with whom the bishop has a special association. Within that setting, there are those with special responsibilities such as deans, archdeacons and rural deans. Also at the same level is the diocesan council, another team elected by the diocesan synod and charged with making difficult decisions. They are served by a small but vital team of administrative staff.

A bishop is also part of a team represented by the national house or college of bishops under the leadership of the primate. When problems loom large at local level, it is comforting to learn that they do not vary greatly from diocese to diocese, and indeed from country to country. The house of bishops is no doubt viewed in a variety of ways, depending on one's predisposition. For my own part, I would want to stress the supportive role it plays for those whose lot is cast in isolation, as is the case with each bishop.

The consecration service took place in Christ Church Cathedral, Dublin, on St Brigid's Day, 1 February 1988. As so often happens on such occasions, memories are jumbled. I was deeply conscious of the supportive presence of so many episcopal colleagues, both active and retired, and Dr McAdoo's sermon on the theme of the Good Shepherd. Conscious too of being part of an ancient ceremony, and the basis that continuity supplies. The presence of the President, Dr Hillery, lent a national significance to the occasion, while the presence of Bishop George Henderson (Argyll and The Isles) was a reminder of the wider Church dimension. The Lord Mayor of Cork was represented by Mr Dan Wallace, and the Roman Catholic community by the Auxiliary Bishop of Cork and Ross, the Most Rev. John Buckley. Weatherwise, storm and rain were the order of the day, and for those travelling from the extremities of Cork, Cloyne and Ross, the journey to Dublin was hazardous to say the least.

Christ Church Cathedral, like St Fin Barre's, is just about the right size to provide that delightful combination of homeliness and sense of occasion. Fortunately, we were still able to cross the bridge linking the cathedral and the Synod Hall for the reception, and one felt a pang of regret that the general synod members no longer pass the same way.

The setting of the palace in Cork must be one of the most pleasing in the Church of Ireland. Set on a hill, there is a fine view across the city, with St Ann's, Shandon, prominent on the skyline. Through the trees one glimpses the magnificent façade of St Fin Barre's Cathedral, the third cathedral to be built on the site where Cork originated in the seventh century. Set in four-and-a-half acres of ground, the palace dates from 1782 and is characterised by a dry moat. Inside, one is conscious of the upstairs/downstairs character of the building, with a back stairs going from the basement to the top storey without impinging on the main living area. The two public rooms are generous in their proportions and, on occasions, can absorb up to 100 people. Shortly after our arrival, we experienced one such occasion with the annual St Patrick's Day reception for the Lord Mayor and Corporation and various civic leaders.

The grounds form a fitting setting for the house, and a fruitful source of inspiration for the students from the Crawford College of Art and Design nearby. The surrounding roads have an ecclesiastical ring about them with such names as Bishop Street, Dean Street and Gregg Road. The last name is a reminder of a remarkable episcopal dynasty. Bishop John Gregg was in office when the present cathedral was built. He was succeeded as bishop by his brother, Robert, while his grandson, John Allen Fitzgerald Gregg, was destined to become one of the foremost archbishops in the Church of Ireland this century.

The United Diocese of Cork, Cloyne and Ross is, to all intents and purposes, coterminous with the county of Cork, extending approximately 120 miles from east to west and 50 miles from north to south. Cork and Ross were united under one bishop in 1582, while Cloyne was added in 1835. Although it is administered by one synod and council, there are three cathedrals – St Fin Barre's, designed by William Burges and described by Sir John Betjeman as an architectural gem; St Colman's, Cloyne, much associated with the philosopher, George Berkeley; and St Fachtna's, Ross, within whose precincts a bishop's daughter was once murdered!

Of the total population of the city and county of Cork (415,464), only 8,222 are Church of Ireland, that is, 2 per cent. Of these, 50 per cent live within 15 miles of Cork city, and the remainder are unevenly spread, representing up to 15 per cent of the population in pockets of west Cork and 1 per cent in north Cork. In recent years, the Church of Ireland population trend has been to hold its own, but it is characterised by a general movement to conurbation. Socially, it represents a cross-section of the population, with farmers and small business owners found in the rural areas. Ireland as a whole has the highest house-owning percentage in the EC, and this is reflected in the Church of Ireland population.

Unemployment, often leading to emigration, is a national phenomenon, and Cork is no exception, although this is not always reflected in the Church of Ireland population. This is not to deny that certain categories are affected more than others, for example graduates and nurses. In a country where 50 per cent of the population is under twenty-five years of age, it would be strange if we as a diocese did not experience some of the problem.

In terms of actual employment, those in rural areas are mostly self-employed, while those in the city are usually either employers or engaged in service areas such as teaching, nursing and as secretaries.

Other Protestant traditions are comparatively small in number, except for localised groups of Methodists and Presbyterians with whom there are good ecumenical relations. There are a certain number of house churches, often drawing their strength from former Roman Catholics, and a Baptist church in Cork city which attracts many young people. Unlike the situation in the other three home countries, the Baptist Church in Ireland has tended to remain outside the ecumenical context. There is also a small community of Quakers.

For some time, the diocese has been in the process of implementing a rationalisation programme with regard to churches. In one sense, this has been going on since disestablishment. For example, in 1871 there were 171 churches in the diocese. However, since the mid-1970s it has been gathering momentum, beginning with the amalgamation of parishes and a planned reduction in manpower. There are now 24 parochial units and provision for 23 stipendiary clergy, one youth chaplain, one stipendiary lay worker, and one church army officer. The aim is to reduce the number of buildings to 70. This compares with 1970 when there were 41 parochial units, 111 churches and 45 clergy.

Shortly after my arrival, the diocesan council decided to invite the Commission on Church Buildings to survey the diocese. This body, set up by the general synod in 1986 and given absolute powers, had as its brief to determine the number of churches required for the worship, work and witness of the Church of Ireland in the specific diocese to which it was invited. It consisted of representatives from every diocese in Ireland, but naturally the local representatives did not act in their own dioceses.

Although the commission had a positive brief, it was inevitable that it would be interpreted by many in negative terms of church closures. Such was the case when the final report was issued in the summer of 1989. Within the Church of Ireland psyche there is a great attachment to buildings, and this soon became very evident. However, through the ensuing trauma, there has emerged for some people a deeper understanding of the role of the Church, the nature of worship and the possibilities of exciting developments for surplus buildings. There has also been much hurt and this has centred not just on the actual closures but on the overall approach to the problem which, in many cases, was viewed as authoritarian. In the vast majority of cases, the need to reduce the number of church buildings was accepted, but there was general agreement that the consultative process required strengthening, and those at local level are justified in expecting rational explanations for decisions taken.

There are major problems resulting from church closures, apart altogether from the human trauma. Like a house unoccupied, a church unused soon falls a victim to vandalism, and dotted throughout the countryside are buildings which do nothing for the reputation of the Church of Ireland. There are few sadder sights than an ecclesiastical eyesore. As already indicated, there are some exciting proposals such as a stained-glass museum, a retreat and educational centre, and at least two heritage centres. In Cork city one church is used to house archives. But there is a limit to the desirable uses to which redundant churches can be put, and some of the churches are located in isolated areas not conducive to development. Part of the bill setting up the commission provides for money to be available for the demolition of churches. While this is always an option, it is not one readily acceptable to parishioners, and who can blame them, especially if their association with the building goes back for generations? Although there are legal implications for the Representative Body as trustees, I believe it would be a sensitive approach if money could be made available for the development of redundant churches, as well as their demolition. It would be a positive approach in an area of much negative reaction. A bill giving effect to this was passed at the 1993 general synod.

Coupled with the disposal of churches is the question of surplus furniture and fittings. Many churches have been adorned and beautified by the generosity of parishioners both past and present, and great sensitivity is needed in the matter. Approached imaginatively this can be an occasion of great joy and an opportunity for the development of inter-Church and parochial links. For example, in one case a bell from a redundant church in Cork has been transported to Tanzania and the project has enriched the life of the whole parish. In another case, an organ from Co. Cork has been reassembled in Co. Donegal much to the delight of the rector who writes:

> This organ, perhaps the smallest pipe organ in Ireland and ideally suited to our needs, was collected and thoroughly overhauled, renovated and rebuilt and installed just a week or so ago. In sound and appearance it is a little gem, and we are absolutely delighted with the result. It was built in 1881 by W. Browne of Dublin and in its present renovated condition it is good for at least a further hundred years or more!

By such means are bonds of fellowship created, and the burden of history, in the shape of excessive churches, becomes the unlikely vehicle for deeper unity.

One particular aspect of this whole problem deserves special mention, and that is the stained glass windows in our churches. Windows are usually designed for a particular purpose in a particular church and, apart altogether from the cost, are not easily transferred. Furthermore, the value of a specific window may not always be appreciated except by an expert. Bearing all this in mind, the diocese decided to have the stained glass in the churches scheduled for closure examined, and a report given by Dr David Lawrence of Canterbury. This brief was then extended by the diocesan council to cover the whole diocese. A comprehensive report which, I understand, is the first of its kind in the Anglican Communion, is awaited with interest. The intimations are that there is some extremely valuable stained glass in the diocese. This places a dual burden of responsibility on the Church authorities: on the one hand, the care of that which is in use, and on the other hand, the future of the glass in redundant churches.

In 1986, before becoming Bishop of Cork, I voted at the general synod for the setting up of the Commission on Church Buildings, together with its terms of reference. I cannot recall anyone voting against the bill, not even those from Cork! Perhaps some of us felt that we would not be affected by it. But history can play funny tricks, and those on the sideline can suddenly find themselves involved in the action. Perhaps in this case the action has had wider implications than were imagined, both personal and practical. Yet, as I reflect on this particular aspect of diocesan life, I am reminded of some words spoken at a recent House of Bishops' retreat, by the conductor, Brother Bernard: 'If we hold on, we may miss what God has now for us today.'

Perhaps the two events I looked forward to with most excitement and apprehension were my first confirmation and ordination. I was conscious that these were specifically episcopal duties and, in performing them, I was going to the heart of my work as a bishop. The first confirmation service was in Midleton church, when I had the privilege of confirming, with others, my archdeacon's daughter and the Dean of Cloyne's son. My first ordinations were on Sunday, 26 June, when Mr John Fenning and Mr Peter Hanna were made deacons to serve in the auxiliary ministry. On St Peter's Day, the Rev. Michael Burrows was raised to the priesthood in St Fin Barre's Cathedral. He was an appropriate candidate as his father, Canon Walter Burrows, had conducted the pre-ordination retreat for the class of 1953, thirty-five years earlier.

Within six months of consecration, I was fortunate in being able to attend the twelfth Lambeth Conference at the University of Kent, which was the largest ever held – 518 bishops compared to 76 at the first. The report, *The Truth Shall Make You Free*, gives some indication of the scope of the conference, but it cannot really convey the sense of fellowship experienced under the chairmanship of the Archbishop of Canterbury, Dr Robert Runcie. I stress this because forebodings of disintegration loomed large in the media before the conference. As it turned out, the formal worship, the group Bible study and the cut and thrust of group discussion and plenary debate all helped to mould the diverse elements into a family in the Spirit. The truth as it was perceived was spoken in love, and accepted in the spirit in which it was uttered, even though there were disagreements.

Two elements were notably different from previous conferences. The members of the Anglican Consultative Council were present, and the breadth of representation (not just episcopal) contributed much to the occasion. Also present were the wives of the bishops, who had their own conference in a nearby school. Their presence was a recognition of the supportive role played by wives at an episcopal level.

For my wife and me it was a memorable learning experience, and invaluable so early on in episcopal life. As one of the newest bishops I was designated a 'baby bishop'. I am not sure how soon one graduates to youth and manhood, but the Lambeth Conference certainly helped in the process.

To return from a Lambeth Conference to diocesan life is like the three apostles coming down from the Mount of Transfiguration to be confronted by the problems of the plain. Not that there weren't problems at Lambeth, especially for the steering committee and others with specialist roles to fulfil, but at diocesan level each bishop has his own areas of concern.

In addition to the matters already alluded to, there is the ever present difficulty of filling vacant parishes. Comparatively early retirement (now 68), coupled with a reluctance to serve in many rural areas (a type of Pale mentality), means that many parishes are left vacant for lengthy periods. While this may occasionally have the effect of bringing a parish to life as parishioners begin to utilise their gifts, in general, it is not to be recommended. 'A ship without a captain' is how the situation has been described to me. It may, in fact, force the Church of Ireland to take a long, hard look at the question of ministry and the most appropriate models for such areas.

Finance is never far from the diocesan agenda, and as a result of the report of the Clergy Remunerations and Benefits Committee (CRAB), stipends have been increased. In Cork, a system of pooling has been in operation for many years, whereby the operational cost of the diocese is divided on a per capita basis throughout the parishes. By means of this, the strong support the weak. But there must come a saturation point and the only substantial saving possible is in manpower. Hence, there is all the more need to look at traditional models.

Any rethinking must take into account the basic full-time nature of ministry, and the twenty-four hour 'on call' needs that must be serviced in hospitals and parish. Add to these such things as teaching responsibilities, and community and ecumenical representation – and one begins to sense the difficulties if the full-time stipendiary ministry has to be slimmed down too drastically. Nor is it just a matter of statistics. There are deeply ingrained expectations on the part of laity, and any alteration of policy must be coupled with an education of attitude at grass-roots level.

A similar type of education is needed if the Church of Ireland is to respond to another recommendation in the CRAB report, that referring to sabbaticals. Nothing is more guaranteed to revive a flagging ministry than a planned period of spiritual and intellectual refreshment. It is an area sadly neglected in Ireland, and may well have a bearing on the subject of clergy stress. In many other professions it is now a regular feature of employment, to the benefit of all concerned.

One of the boom areas of activity at present is that associated with alternative medicine, and closely linked with this is the New Age movement which poses a challenge to orthodox religion. Many newcomers to West Cork are caught up with this modern phenomenon, and as a diocese we are fortunate in having one of our clergy, the Rev. Chris Peters, who has made a special study of the movement. His experience and expertise have been widely used in helping people to come to grips with a very diffused philosophy of life. It highlights the need for a sound grounding in basic Christianity, which in turn leads on to the recurring theme of youth and their lack of interest in the Church. If there is this lack of interest, then surely we must ask – why? Could it be that, with all our structures, we are not satisfying the fundamental spiritual needs of our young people, and with the natural adventure of youth they are looking elsewhere? It is one of the more perplexing questions in Church life. In few other areas is more finance expended and are more work hours contributed, and yet the end result seems to be a continuing problem. Perhaps it has to do with the quick turnover of clients and the need to start afresh each year.

These were the type of questions addressed at the first International Conference of Young Anglicans held in Belfast in January 1988. A second conference was planned for 1993 but, due to lack of financial commitment world-wide, it has had to be cancelled. That in itself may say something about the role of youth in the Anglican Communion!

On the domestic level, June 1988 saw the appointment of a new chief officer and secretary for the Representative Body, in the person of Mr Robert Sherwood; while at the general synod the Primate dwelt on the role of the Church in mass communication. At the same synod, a committee was set up to look at the whole question of clergy under stress.

In 1989, the Primate appointed Lady Carswell as his assessor, the first occasion on which a lady had acted in that capacity. In his presidential address, referring to the situation in Northern Ireland, he said that the main struggle is to win the hearts and minds of those who permit terrorism to continue. During the same session of synod, the Church of Ireland Youth Council (CIYC) was established as a separate body, having previously been under the umbrella of the general synod board of education.

The following year was marked by the sudden death of Cardinal Tomás Ó Fiaich, and the retirement of Archbishop Runcie who was replaced by Bishop George Carey. The general synod was dominated by the debate and vote on the ordination of women.

General synod returned to Belfast in 1991 which also saw the primates of the Anglican Communion meeting in Ireland. As they travelled throughout the country, our island Church was enabled to see itself as part of a world-wide body with renewed vision. 'Relevance' was the key word in Archbishop Eames' presidential address. He urged the Church at all levels to preface its activities with the question: 'Is it relevant?' In the course of the address he gave the interesting statistic that during the previous year approximately 3,000 candidates were confirmed.

During the synod, two select committees were set up reflecting the deeply felt concerns of members; one to deal with marriage and the other with the admission of those baptised, but unconfirmed, to Holy Communion. However, the item that provoked most debate and subsequent controversy was a motion proposed by the Bishop of Tuam (the Rt Rev. John Neill) and seconded by the Very Rev. John Paterson, that a statement of the House of Bishops issued to the standing committee in April 1991 be received and affirmed by the synod. The statement was as follows:

> In May 1990, the General Synod of the Church of Ireland passed the Bill enabling women to be ordained to the Priesthood and the Episcopate. Recognising that the decision represented a development in the Ministry of the Church of Ireland and that some Church members, both clerical and lay, have genuinely felt that this change has significantly affected their relationship to the Church of Ireland, it is hereby affirmed that they should suffer no discrimination or loss of respect in their membership or in their Ministry by reason of their *bona fide* held views, nor should such views constitute any impediment to the exercise of Ministry in the Church of Ireland.

The statement was intended to reflect the pastoral concern of the House of Bishops, and in one sense need only have been reported to the synod. It soon became obvious that the House was divided on the question of affirmation. Some speakers felt that to do so would give the statement a certain legislative standing. By way of compromise, and in order to rescue the situation, that experienced parliamentarian, the Bishop of Kilmore (the Rt Rev. Gilbert Wilson), proposed that the words 'hereby affirmed' be deleted. This was seconded by the Very Rev. J.A. Fair and passed on a vote of 242 For and 170 Against. So the statement was received. This dilution of the original proposal resulted in the resignation of Dean Paterson as a secretary of the general synod.

While synod is at liberty to determine its own *modus operandi*, I believe that its action in this instance in no way diminishes the pastoral concern and obligation of the House of Bishops.

1991 marked the bicentenary of the death of John Wesley,

and the ecumenical spirit of the age was reflected in a motion passed at synod giving thanks to Almighty God for 'the service, preaching, ministry and influence of the Rev. John Wesley, priest and evangelist'.

Educational clouds were looming on the horizon when the general synod met in 1992. An introduction to the Green Paper (*Education for a Changing World*) had been issued, and the paper itself was awaited with trepidation. When it arrived it became clear that the future for many Protestant schools was uncertain, both in terms of survival and management structures. Innumerable hours have been spent in addressing the issues raised, and submissions made by a variety of bodies to the Department of Education, including a comprehensive analysis from the Republic of Ireland Committee of the General Synod Board of Education. The frequent changes at ministerial level have not made for consistency of attitude, while the current financial climate adds to the uncertainty, given the recurring theme of financial availability in the Green Paper itself.

In addition to education, two other subjects in particular were the occasion of intense debate – the future of the Adelaide Hospital and the remarriage of divorced persons. The former centred on maintaining a liberal medical ethic wherever the Adelaide might be, while the latter resulted in leave being given to introduce a bill in 1993 for the regulation of marriage discipline in the Church of Ireland to allow for the remarriage of divorced persons, with various safeguards. The voting on this issue was comprehensively in favour – Clergy: 142 For, 17 Against; Laity: 209 For, 19 Against. At the 1993 general synod the bill was withdrawn at the third reading. Members were unhappy with the introduction of a penitential section, and a motion was passed requesting the standing committee to appoint a committee to consider the questions raised during the debate on the bill and to report to the 1994 general synod.

On a less dramatic but nonetheless significant level, 1992 saw the synod pass a bill introducing a revised ordinal after a gestation period of some years. This brings our ordinal into line with most of the other provinces of the Anglican Communion, and completes the revision of the major services in the Church of Ireland. If worship be at the heart of the Church's life, then what more fitting climax could there be to the last forty years?

In 1953, there were eleven deacons ordained in the Church of Ireland. Arithmetically speaking, that means 440 years of service in and to the Church. Service offered in a variety of circumstances – in inner city and suburbia, in rural pastures, in strife-torn areas of Northern Ireland, in locations far beyond the Church of Ireland, embracing both hemispheres, as full- and part-time chaplains in a variety of institutions. Time would fail to tell and many books could not contain the catalogue of ministry embraced by those 440 years. And even if the books could all be written, they would not begin to take account of the ripples in the pool.

Index